The Essential Guide to Interpersonal Communication

Dan O'Hair
University of Oklahoma

Mary O. Wiemann
Santa Barbara City College

BEDFORD / ST. MARTIN'S
Boston ♦ New York

Manufactured in the United States of America.

3 2 1 0 9
l k j i h g

For information, write: Bedford/St. Martin's, 75 Arlington Street, Boston,
MA 02116   (617-399-4000)

ISBN: 0-312-45195-4

PREFACE

The Essential Guide to Interpersonal Communication is a versatile supplement for students who need a brief, topical introduction to key concepts in interpersonal communication. It has been designed as a flexible option for use in a variety of speech courses, including introduction to communication classes that do not use a traditional full-size text, "public speaking plus" classes that concentrate on public speaking but also include units on interpersonal communication along with other communication topics, and any class where instructors want to give students a brief but thorough introduction to interpersonal communication. Developed primarily for use with O'Hair, Stewart, and Rubenstein's *A Speaker's Guidebook* and *A Pocket Guide to Public Speaking*, it can be used as well with a wide variety of communication texts.

The Essential Guide to Interpersonal Communication helps students identify and understand core issues in interpersonal communication quickly and effectively through an approach that combines a solid foundation in communication theory with a clear emphasis on student skill acquisition. Topic coverage includes:

- An overview of communication theory (Chapter 1)
- Discussions of the definition of interpersonal communication, the functions of interpersonal communication, and the elements of successful interpersonal messages (Chapter 1)
- The building blocks of interpersonal communication: self-concept, perception, language, nonverbal communication, and listening (Chapter 2)
- Developing and maintaining interpersonal relationships: the roles of relationships and the individual, goals and motivations in relationships, types of relationships, the stages of relationships, expectations of relationships, and the costs and rewards of relationships (Chapter 3)
- Understanding and managing interpersonal conflicts: conditions producing conflict, thinking of conflict as inevitable and healthy, and specific tools for effective conflict management (Chapter 4)

FEATURES

The approach and content of this text are based on the extensive experience of Dan O'Hair and Mary Wiemann teaching interpersonal communication in the classroom, and the pedagogy is based on the successful innovations developed in *A Speaker's Guidebook.*

Throughout *The Essential Guide,* you will find useful *checklists,* offering step-by-step directions, assessment checks, and content review checks. Widely praised by reviewers for their precision and conciseness, these checklists help students understand key concepts and assess their own learning.

Compelling features throughout the text highlight issues vital to interpersonal communicators. *Interpersonal Communication in Cultural Perspective* boxes help students understand the cultural requirements of speech situations. They feature topics such as perceptions of U.S. culture and cultural differences in saying "hello" nonverbally. *Ethically Speaking* boxes emphasize the importance of ethics in interpersonal communication situations and include such topics as responsibility in the transactional communication process.

This booklet is available either as a stand-alone text; or packaged with *A Speaker's Guidebook, A Pocket Guide to Public Speaking,* and a number of other Bedford/St. Martin's communication titles including the booklet *The Essential Guide to Group Communication.* Please note that because the booklets have been designed to stand alone, the coverage of communication theory in both *The Essential Guide to Interpersonal Communication* and *The Essential Guide to Group Communication* is identical. For information on these or other Bedford/St. Martin's communication texts, or to contact your local sales representative, please visit our Web site at <bedfordstmartins.com>.

CONTENTS

Preface   iii

1 *A First Look at Interpersonal Communication*   *1*

What Is Communication?   1
   Communication Is Symbolic   *2*
   Communication Is a Shared Code   *2*
   Communication Is Linked to Culture   *3*
   Communication Is Intentional   *3*
      BOX: INTERPERSONAL COMMUNICATION IN CULTURAL PERSPECTIVE:
      Comparing Communication Norms   4
   Communication Is Mediated   *5*
   Communication Is Transactional   *5*
      BOX: ETHICALLY SPEAKING: Your Ethical Responsibility in the
      Transactional Communication Process   6
What Is Interpersonal Communication?   6
Functions of Interpersonal Communication   6
   Communicating to Seek Control   *7*
   Communicating to Gain Acceptance   *8*
   Communicating to Achieve a Goal   *8*
What Determines Success in Interpersonal Communication?   9
   Taking a Process Approach to Determining Success   *9*
   Appropriate and Effective Behavior   *9*

2 *The Building Blocks of Interpersonal Communication*   *11*

Self-Concept   11
Perception   12
      BOX: INTERPERSONAL COMMUNICATION IN CULTURAL PERSPECTIVE:
      Perceptions of U.S. Culture   13
      ✓ CHECKLIST: Improving Your Perception Skills   14
Language   14
      ✓ CHECKLIST: Determining the Appropriate Level of
         Abstraction   15
   The Language of Relationship Definition   *16*
   The Language of Intimacy and Distance   *16*
   The Language of Control   *17*
Nonverbal Communication   18
   Appearance and Artifacts   *18*

v

Gestures and Body Movements   18
Facial Expressions and Eye Behavior   19
   BOX: *Interpersonal Communication in Cultural Perspective:*
      Cultural Differences in Saying Hello Nonverbally   20
Paralanguage   21
Touch   22
Space   22
Time Orientation   23
Scents and Smells   23
Listening   24
   ✓ CHECKLIST: Strategies for Applying the Four Functions of
      Listening   25

3 *Developing and Maintaining Interpersonal Relationships*   **28**
   ✓ CHECKLIST: Thinking about Your Own Experiences with
      Interpersonal Communication   28
The Role of Relationships in Interpersonal Communication   28
The Role of the Individual   29
The Role of Relational Knowledge   29
Goals and Motivations for Relationship Development   30
Interpersonal Attraction   30
Physical Proximity   30
Alleviating Loneliness   31
Stimulation   31
Achieving Goals   31
Types of Relationships   32
Friendship   32
Family   34
   ✓ CHECKLIST: Improving Family Relations   34
Stages of Relationships   35
The Initiation Stage   36
The Exploration Stage   36
The Intensification Stage   36
The Stabilization Stage   37
   ✓ CHECKLIST: Paths to Stable Relationships   37
   ✓ CHECKLIST: Strategies for Maintaining Intimacy   38
   ✓ CHECKLIST: Strategies for Establishing Effective Love
      Relationships   39
The Decline Stage   39
The Termination Stage   40
Expectations of Relationship Development   42
Expectations about Relationships   43
Expectations about Relational Partners   43

Knowledge, Motives, and Expectations   44

Costs and Rewards of Relationships   44

4 *Understanding and Managing Interpersonal Conflicts*   46

Conditions Producing Interpersonal Conflict   46
Incompatible Goals   46
Unrealistic Expectations   47
Differing Rates of Relational Growth   47
Inaccurate Perceptions and Attributions   47
Cultural Differences in Handling Conflict   48

Conflict as Inevitable and Healthy Communication   48
Decision Making   49
Enjoyment of Conflict   50
Relational Growth   50
Saving Time   51

A Model of Effective Conflict Management   51
Prelude   52
Assessment   55
Engagement   57
Action   58
Decision   61
     ✓ CHECKLIST: Effective Bargaining Strategies   61
Reflection   62
     ✓ CHECKLIST: Steps Toward Effective Interpersonal
       Communication   64

Glossary   65

Notes   69

A First Look 1
at Interpersonal Communication

Since we all participate in interpersonal relationships, we cannot avoid communicating with other people. Sometimes that communication is successful, and sometimes it is not. Often, our success or failure depends on how well we understand the dynamics of interpersonal relationships. As we become aware of the factors that influence relationships, we are better able to develop, maintain, or terminate relationships in our own lives. In addition, we are able to develop the social skills needed in formal as well as informal contexts.

The quality of your life depends directly on your ability to communicate with others—a process known as *interpersonal communication*. Whether you realize it or not, you communicate in order to accomplish social tasks and to coordinate physical ones. In the process, you not only create and define interpersonal relationships, you also modify and dissolve them.

The better you understand the interpersonal communication process, the more likely you will be to use your communication skills appropriately and effectively—and the more likely you will be to create satisfying, productive, and meaningful interpersonal relationships in your life.

WHAT IS COMMUNICATION?

In order to improve your own knowledge and understanding of interpersonal communication, you first need to understand the basic communication process. **Communication** is a process that is defined by six characteristics:

- Communication is *symbolic.*
- Communication is a *shared code.*
- Communication is linked to *culture.*
- Communication is *intentional.*
- Communication is *mediated.*
- Communication is *transactional.*

Behavior that clearly possesses all of these characteristics (to one degree or another) is *communication* and can be analyzed as such. Keep in mind, however, that the line between what is communication and what is not can sometimes be blurry. Some messages are more obviously communicative than others. For example, when six-year-old Ellie sticks her tongue out at Jake, that's communication that is very purposeful; but when twenty-one-year-old Sara makes one-second eye contact with Alan across the room, her intention to communicate is less clear.

It is useful, therefore, for us to be able to analyze messages in terms of these characteristics, so that we can understand why communication problems occur and how we might solve them. Using this approach will help you to evaluate the various messages you receive on a daily basis. Let's take a look at each of these six characteristics in detail.

COMMUNICATION IS SYMBOLIC

Behavior is symbolic when it has an arbitrary relationship to an object. **Symbols** are arbitrary constructions that are related to the objects to which they refer. The stronger the connection between symbol and object, the clearer the intended meaning.

The most **symbolic behavior** is language. Every language is a code that allows those who know it to transform speech into meaningful messages. There is no particular reason why the arbitrary transcription of the letters T-R-E-E should represent a very large variety of plant form. But in our code, American English, it does.

Although spoken language is the primary form of symbolic behavior in our culture, nonverbal behavior can also be symbolic. Hand gestures, in particular, may have symbolic properties. For example, joining the thumb and forefinger in a circle while extending the other three fingers means "okay" in middle-class U.S. culture. Gestures of this sort, "autonomous gestures,"[1] operate in much the same way as language. That is to say, we do not need words to know what they mean.

COMMUNICATION IS A SHARED CODE

In order for communication to take place, the participants must share the **code** (the set of symbol-meaning relationships) used to **encode** and **decode** messages.

Speaking a common language is the most obvious example of sharing a communication code. Keep in mind, however, that although we tend to assume that because people share a language code they share common meanings for the symbols they use, this is clearly not the case. For example, American travelers to and from England are frequently surprised (and amused) that the same words refer to different things in the two versions of the English language. A British person in a U.S. drugstore asking for a rubber would be sent to the pharmaceutical counter for a condom rather than to the stationery aisle for an eraser.

Keep in mind, however, that a symbol can take on new meaning if at least two people agree that it will have that meaning for them. Social groups use this technique to establish their uniqueness and to create boundaries between themselves and the "outside" world.

Speaking a common language is the most obvious example of sharing a communication code, but it is not the only one. Each culture also shares specific meanings for gestures, tones of voice, and facial expressions. Some aspects of these codes cross cultural boundaries, making them especially powerful communication vehicles. Facial expressions of surprise, fear, disgust, anger, happiness, and sadness seem to have universal meanings.[2] Thus, they allow people from different cultures to understand each other's most basic feelings, even when they cannot speak the same language.

COMMUNICATION IS LINKED TO CULTURE

If you've ever traveled to a different country or even through the different neighborhoods of a city, you know that communication is difficult to separate from culture. We use the term **culture** to refer to the shared beliefs, values, and practices of a group of people. A group's culture includes the language or languages used by group members as well as the norms and rules about how behavior can appropriately be displayed and how it should be understood.

The strongest connection between communication and culture is language. People from different cultures usually speak different languages, which are often unintelligible to "strangers." But the communication-culture relationship goes well beyond obvious language differences. Cultural experience and everyday life strongly influence how language influences our interpretation of the world around us.[3] For example, an interior decorator may find it useful, or even necessary, to distinguish among lavender, mauve, burgundy, violet, plum, lilac, magenta, amethyst, and heliotrope. For many of us, however, these fine distinctions are unimportant; purple is purple!

Our nonverbal behavior also is wrapped up in culture. Different cultures use and interpret time and space differently.[4] In Mediterranean cultures, for instance, men tend to stand very close together, frequently touching each other during conversation. In North Atlantic cultures, the appropriate conversational distance is generally about 3 feet — and, in case you hadn't noticed, men seldom touch each other during social conversation except when they shake hands in greeting.

COMMUNICATION IS INTENTIONAL

A behavior must be **intentional** to be communicative; that is, the communicator must exhibit a high level of consciousness or purposefulness while encoding messages. If you see me do something or hear me say something I did not intend for you to see or hear, did I communicate with you? Am I responsible

INTERPERSONAL COMMUNICATION IN CULTURAL PERSPECTIVE

Comparing Communication Norms

Many cultural rules and norms are observed unconsciously and are not thought about until they are ignored or broken. That is, you take the rules and norms of your culture for granted, you typically follow them, and you expect your communication partners to follow them. But when you move from one culture (or from one subculture) to another, rules that were taken for granted and behaviors that seemed automatic may become the source of interpersonal difficulties.

In order to better understand (1) the nature of communication rules and norms and (2) the problems that "strangers" to a culture encounter, try your hand at the exercise below.

Spend 15 to 30 minutes in a familiar environment (preferably your home or dorm) observing the communication behaviors and patterns of those around you from the perspective of a visitor from a different culture. Do not take anything for granted. Do not indicate to your subjects that you are observing their behavior. Conduct your observations with respect for your subjects.

Record the results of your observations, paying special attention to how you understood what was appropriate behavior. Now, ask yourself:

- What rules and norms can I list?
- How did I identify these rules and norms?
- Do they apply to more than one "culture" (that is, are they peculiar to the context I observed or can they be generalized to other, similar contexts)?
- How does my experience compare with those of my classmates?
- Were conflicting or different norms "discovered" by different people from either the same or different "cultures"?
- How would the people around me react if I had violated these norms?
- How could a person from one culture best discover a rule in another culture?
- How can (or should) people from one culture adhere to another culture's rule when that rule violates a rule from their own culture?

to you for what I did or said in the same way as if I had intentionally formulated a message and transmitted it to you? Can you stop yourself from blushing when you don't want to blush?

While communication is sometimes characterized by behavior that is primarily (if not totally) symbolic and intentional and has a cognitive basis, other times our communication is based on emotional and physiological considerations, characterized by a widely shared code that has few, if any, cultural boundaries and is spontaneous.[5] This distinction can be seen as one of *giving* information versus one of *giving off* information.[6] The practical importance of the distinction is that we tend to see a person as more accountable when he or she consciously or purposefully gives information to someone else than when the recipient gleans information from observation or overhearing.

This is not to say that information *given off* is unimportant. In fact, it may be evaluated as more honest because the person giving off the information did not have the opportunity to censor or package it. It is useful to note, however, that while some messages transmitted through the emotional communication system are highly reliable and easily interpreted (e.g., emotional displays like grief and anger), most are ambiguous and open to a variety of interpretations (What does a flushed face mean?). Generally this sort of information can be interpreted through contextual cues, and even then it may be a judgment call that is open to question.

Effective communication requires a sensitivity to the fact that both your intended and unintended messages have an impact on the people around you. Keep in mind that the intended meaning (if there is one) of your behavior is not always as clearly expressed or as accurately received as you would like.

COMMUNICATION IS MEDIATED

Communication requires a **medium**—a vehicle to transport or carry the symbols. In face-to-face interaction, the vehicle is the air through which the sound and light waves travel. However, communication doesn't need to be face to face to be effective; it can be maintained through a variety of media. Long-distance relationships are becoming ever more common. As we move away from face-to-face contact and technology intervenes between us and our **audience**, the characteristics and the social impact of our messages change, sometimes in very subtle ways. With the advent of the information superhighway, which already merges television cable, telephone, and online computer services in the home, we are likely to see an increase in several types of long-distance relationships. These relationships include not only those between parents and children, siblings, and close friends, but also commuter marriages and even "telecommuting"—arrangements in which the employee is connected to the workplace by computer and audio/video media and so can go to work without leaving home. (Many students text-message one another while sitting in class.)

COMMUNICATION IS TRANSACTIONAL

Communication is **transactional**; that is, two or more people exchange **sender** and **receiver** roles, and their messages are dependent on and influenced by

ETHICALLY SPEAKING

Your Ethical Responsibility in the Transactional Communication Process

When you engage others in communication, you are not only attempting to influence them in some way, you are also opening yourself to influence by others. We are all involved in the transactional process of communication. Keep in mind that all parties to an interaction are responsible for its outcome and have a hand in whether individual and relational goals are met. Whether you are talking with your significant other, a parent, a work group in a class, or the audience of a public speech, you share responsibility for the outcome of the interaction. The burden of responsibility is usually more or less equally distributed, depending on the communication situation. In some situations, like public speaking, the speaker tends to assume most of the responsibility and is seen as the person attempting to influence the audience. But even in this apparently lopsided situation, the audience still retains a good deal of influence. The audience's power is most obvious when applause or catcalls interrupt a speech.

those of their partner(s). This exchange can be immediate, as in a conversation, or delayed, as in the case of mass media messages or e-mail exchanges.

We have looked at the six major characteristics of communication. Let us now turn our attention to the primary reason for constructing communicative messages in the first place: achieving satisfying relationships in which we can accomplish our personal and interpersonal goals.

WHAT IS INTERPERSONAL COMMUNICATION?

Now that we have explored the nature of *communication*, let's take a look at what *interpersonal communication* means. **Interpersonal communication** is the process of two or three people exchanging messages in order to share meaning, create understanding, and develop relationships.

Now let's look at what functions interpersonal communication serves.

FUNCTIONS OF INTERPERSONAL COMMUNICATION

In this book, we take a **functional perspective** on interpersonal communication that focuses on what kinds of communication behaviors work for people, and why they work, in various situations. In this perspective, interpersonal communication is considered **outcome-oriented**, meaning that we do things with some purpose in mind—whether conscious or subconscious. Research has shown that our interpersonal communication behaviors can be clustered into three different types of such purposes or outcomes:

- Control
- Affiliation
- Goal Achievement

COMMUNICATING TO SEEK CONTROL

Control—the ability of one person to not only influence another person, but also influence the manner in which their relationship is conducted—is probably the most important of these three purposes. Note that *control* is not the same as *dominance* (although one person may be dominant) nor does control have to be used in a negative way. Control is a necessary part of every relationship, including marital, boss-worker, parent-child, doctor-patient, lecturer-audience, and even friend-friend. In fact, control is a defining characteristic of every relationship.

The distribution of control is negotiated between relational partners. The more control one person has, the less the other(s) has—for example, if your boss takes 60 percent control of a communication situation, that leaves you with only 40 percent control. This is known as a **zero-sum matter**—a situation in which the more control one party has, the less control the other party has. The distribution of control in an interpersonal relationship can be shared equally, or one partner can hold a high level of control while the other partner holds a lower level of control.

In social relationships, people expect control to be distributed approximately equally. The exact distribution of control in interpersonal relationships is worked out communicatively—by the way people talk with each other, how they structure their conversations (including their timing), and by the content of the conversations. Satisfaction or happiness in interpersonal communication is not solely dependent on how control is distributed within a relationship; another important factor is the way in which the person in control exercises his or her control.

This negotiation takes place in all relationships, from the most informal and unstructured to the most formal and structured. And keep in mind that in many relationships, you expect, if not demand, that your partner(s) have a larger or smaller share of control than you do. Along with the control goes responsibility for the relationship and various tasks relevant to the relationship. For example, as a new employee at a bank, Manny looks to his manager, Sally, for direction and advice about how to do his job well. He expects to be told what to do and how to do it. The lopsided control distribution is appropriate and meets both Manny's and Sally's expectations of their job responsibilities. Thus, it should lead to satisfaction for both of them with regard to this aspect of their relationship. Note that their expectations for their relationship are congruent: Both expect Sally to exercise more control.

COMMUNICATING TO GAIN ACCEPTANCE

In our interpersonal relationships, we seek **affiliation**—feelings for one another, ranging from love (high positive affiliation) to hate (high negative affiliation)—from our communication partners. The more intimate and personal the relationship, the more we expect our partner(s) to feel the same amount of affiliation for us as we do for them. Unlike control, affiliation is not a zero-sum matter—that is, all parties to a relationship can each have a high level of affiliation, a low level of affiliation, or an equal level of affiliation for one another.

Of course, not all communication partners have the same feelings—whether positive or negative—about each other all the time. For this reason, the expression of affiliation must be negotiated. At times you might find it desirable or strategic to hide your feelings for another person. For example, you might not want to show your feelings about a potential dating partner until you find out whether that person is interested in you.

COMMUNICATING TO ACHIEVE A GOAL

The third primary function of communication, **goal achievement**, refers to focusing attention on the task at hand in order to achieve one's goal. Communication that is highly goal- or task-oriented focuses on getting the job done. In unstructured interpersonal relationships, it is useful to think of maintenance of the relationship as the goal toward which both parties should be oriented. In more formal situations, however, the goal may include completing an interview or participating in a public speaking event.

Like the control and affiliation, the goal achievement is negotiable among the communication partners. The task agreed upon during a meeting or get-together can shift during the course of the meeting. For example, a department meeting called by the manager to discuss the production schedule can become a forum for employees to voice their complaints about having to work overtime. Furthermore, communication partners often have competing tasks, and they have to deal with the allocation of time and attention to each of them. For example, students who are assigned to do a group project often have to allocate their time between "being friends" and "getting the project completed/getting a good grade." It can be a challenge to accomplish both tasks in a satisfactory manner.

WHAT DETERMINES SUCCESS
IN INTERPERSONAL COMMUNICATION?

We have seen *what* communication and interpersonal communication are, and *why* we communicate, but now let's take a look at *how* we can go about determining whether our communication efforts are successful.

It is important to remember that success in communication is typically a subjective experience. However, one of two approaches can be applied to assess successful communication:

- **Analyzing the success of the final outcome**, in which we measure the product of a communicative interchange. This approach tends to center around "winning" vs. "losing" and shows little concern for or attention to the way in which the **outcome** was achieved.

- **Analyzing the success of the process**, which measures the way in which the communicative interchange is conducted. In this approach, what is said (and how)—known as the **process**—take on greater significance, although the final outcome is still considered as a factor in determining success or failure. From the process perspective, it is better to optimize outcomes for all communicators than to maximize outcomes for one.

For our purposes, we will take a process approach as our model for determining the relative success or failure of a communicative interaction.

TAKING A PROCESS APPROACH TO DETERMINING SUCCESS

One of the best ways to assess success from the process approach is to look at **mutual satisfaction**. Sometimes winning isn't the most important thing—especially when long-term interpersonal relationships are involved! Geoff may win most of the arguments he has with Betsy, but she increasingly sees him as stubborn and uncaring—a view that may eventually cause her to leave him.

When a communication interaction optimizes outcomes for both partners (rather than maximizing outcomes for one partner at the expense of the other), we say that it is behavior that is *appropriate* and *effective*, and that the communication interaction is a success. Let's explore each of these aspects of determining success in interpersonal communication.

APPROPRIATE AND EFFECTIVE BEHAVIOR

Behavior is **appropriate** when it meets the expectations of:

- one's specific communication partner,
- other people in one's immediate presence, and

- the demands of the situation.

In almost all situations, cultural norms and rules set the standards for expectations of what is appropriate or inappropriate. In other words, a wide variety of communication behaviors may be considered appropriate in any given interpersonal communication situation.

In informal situations, for example, the expectations of your partner and others will be of primary importance to determining appropriateness. However, as situations become more formal and more structured, what counts as appropriate gets more specific. Consider, for instance, the minimal communication latitude one has in a courtroom or a church.

Keep in mind that the expectations generated by different people and situations can, of course, be in conflict with each other. Which set of expectations you choose to honor and which you decide to ignore can say a great deal about your relationship with your communication partners. Knowing what is appropriate and what is not with a wide variety of audiences and in a wide variety of situations is necessary if you are to be a successful interpersonal communicator.

Communication is considered **effective** if it helps you meet your goals. This may sound obvious and straightforward, but in practice it is not always easy to know which messages will serve us in pursuit of our goals.

Just as you craft your persuasive purpose to best convey the message of a persuasive speech, decisions about how to "design" your interpersonal messages so that they might be most effective for a given situation are complicated by the fact that in many situations you have multiple goals.[7] For example, even though Travis might be in a conflict with Jan and wants to have the conflict resolved in his favor, he still wants Jan to continue to like him.

Some knowledge of your communication partner's expectations and the demands of the situation helps you decide which messages will be relatively more effective than others. In addition, knowing that you have multiple goals and prioritizing them—a task that is not always easy—also helps you construct effective messages.

Keep in mind that successful messages are usually, but not always, *both* appropriate and effective. Given your goals, the audience, and the situation, you might have to choose between messages that are primarily effective but inappropriate, and messages that are appropriate but not particularly effective.

The Building Blocks 2
of Interpersonal Communication

All communication involves the basic processes of self-concept development, perception, language, nonverbal communication, and listening. Skills that we develop in these areas can be applied to a wide range of communication contexts—from two friends speaking to group meetings, to public presentations, to mass communication. We need to be especially aware of our communication processes when we are engaged in intercultural communication. Communication differences based on cultural factors can make it more challenging to appropriately interpret and construct messages. When we have a full repertoire of skills available to us, we are able to select the tactics that are both appropriate and effective in our communication.

SELF-CONCEPT

Think for a moment about who you are. Although you may be able to describe yourself by identifying your status as a college student, son or daughter, spouse, parent, or friend to others, there is much more to the self than these simple descriptors. Your **self-concept** is your awareness and understanding of who you are as interpreted and influenced by your thoughts, actions, abilities, values, goals, and ideals, and by other people. Knowing who you are is essential; without a self-concept, it would be impossible for you to relate to others in the world around you.

How does understanding your self-concept affect your communication with others? From the start, you have certain views of who you are as a communicator (for any situation that involves speaking, interviewing, or just talking with others) and views of yourself in other respects that can also affect your communication. For example, if you feel strongly about the issue of the homeless, you are more likely to communicate in ways that support your viewpoint. You may think of yourself as an effective communicator when it comes to that topic. Moreover, self-concept can be a powerful influence on your communication processes; specifically, it can affect how apprehensive you get in certain communication situations,[1] whether you are willing to interact with others,[2] or how you approach someone with a request (e.g., whether you are meek and timid or strong and confident).

The self has a strong influence on your attitude toward communication. Think about people you know who take great pride in their ability to communicate. Do these people place themselves in situations where they are able to use those skills? Do you know other people who have a less favorable concept of their communication skills and who prefer to stand back while others communicate?

The self influences communication in other ways. The self influences many of the mental operations that eventually affect your communication with others. In other words, your perception of others is the product of how you view yourself.[3] If certain attributes about self, such as honesty or wit, are important to you, you will also see them as important traits for other people. If you think that using profanity makes you appear cheap and vulgar, you are likely to think the same of others when they use such language. As you make decisions about your communication, your self-concept influences how you perceive the communication of others.

PERCEPTION

Have you ever met someone for the first time and immediately thought that you did or did not like that person? Your **perceptions**—the way in which you make sense of the world around you—can create very strong feelings that develop with amazing speed.

Whenever you engage in a conversation, whether it is with a longtime friend or a recent acquaintance, you will encounter numerous, specific bits of information that may influence your perception. For instance, in a leisurely walk across campus, you will likely come across at least one person to whom you say hello. Even in the briefest encounter you will receive input, including the exact words of the message, the person's tone of voice, the facial expression, and the presence or lack of eye contact. When considering the amount of information you receive in even a brief interaction, you might question how it is possible to make accurate perceptions. As effective communicators we must learn to manage all of this information—to make sense of it all. If you think of perception as the process of making sense of your world, you can understand the importance of perception for effective interpersonal communication.

Our ability to organize our perceptions in a meaningful way can be broken down into a three-step process:

- **Selection.** As we go about our lives, we select certain stimuli from the environment around us.
- **Organization.** We organize the stimuli we have selected into meaningful patterns.
- **Interpretation.** We interpret these meaningful patterns, and our interpretation is shaped by our past experiences, assumptions, knowledge, and feelings.

Keep in mind that perception is ongoing, and there is no beginning or ending to the perception process. In fact, these three steps need not even take place in this order. For example, a person's past interpretations can influence future selections and the organization of events that are set into motion. In addition, the perception process is influenced by a number of factors, including physiological characteristics (including the five senses, age, health, etc.), cultural background, social roles (including gender roles, occupational roles, etc.), and self-concept.

INTERPERSONAL COMMUNICATION IN CULTURAL PERSPECTIVE

Perceptions of U.S. Culture

People of different cultures will display behavioral and communication differences, leading to differences in perception. These cultural factors make it necessary for individuals from differerent cultural backgrounds to work harder to achieve effective interpersonal communication. The *Bulletin of the Association for Business Communication* reported the results of a survey that had asked 183 international students from 61 countries about their impressions of U.S. culture. Respondents reported their positive and negative impressions, which indicate some ways we might improve as a host culture. The results are listed below.

Positive Impressions	Negative Impressions
Educational opportunities	Rudeness
Friendly people	Weak family structure
Freedoms	Money consciousness
Career opportunities	Ethnocentricity — arrogant, snobbish people
Living conditions	Prejudice against international people
Organized and clean society	Drugs and alcohol
Lack of government red tape	Crime

Source: M. Cassady, "An International Perspective of the United States," *Bulletin of the Association for Business Communication,* 55 (1992).

The process of perception can be complicated; our perceptions are constantly being evaluated for their accuracy. As an effective communicator, you have to be on the lookout for information that ensures that you are perceiving people, events, and issues accurately.

CHECKLIST

Improving Your Perception Skills

✓ **Always try to verify your perceptions.** Sometimes verifying a perception involves gathering information beyond your own observations. For example, if you notice a classmate sitting near the back of the room who is looking from side to side during a test, your initial perception might be that this person is cheating. However, further observation may reveal that the person is simply trying to work out a stiff neck.

✓ **Resist your natural tendency to fall back on the most obvious influence or explanation for what you observe.** For example, occasionally scuffles break out among players in college and professional basketball games. You may tend to assume that the person who threw the first punch initiated the incident. Frequently, however, a scuffle starts when someone else says or does something that fans do not easily perceive. In these situations, ask yourself whether some information or action might have preceded what you observed. Also, question whether you are aware of the reason that someone did or said something. Adopting this approach to verifying perceptions is difficult at first, for it is much easier to make immediate perceptions and not take the time to check their validity.

✓ **Resist the tendency to rely completely on your very first impressions.** These perceptions often lead to inaccurate conclusions. Consider this example: Todd has a tendency to stutter and to slur his words when excited. When people initially meet Todd, they assume he has a learning disability, so they talk slowly and loudly to him. Todd actually has a speech impediment, but he is of average intelligence and is not hearing impaired. Whenever possible, delay reaction or judgment until you can make further perceptions.

LANGUAGE

Language is a symbol system used to think about and communicate experiences and feelings. Because language is symbolic in nature, it is not a precise science; it is the meaning people attach to language that gives language its power.

Language operates at many levels of *abstraction*. You can speak about virtually anyone or anything in a very specific way or a very general way. You can talk so broadly that no one knows what you are talking about ("Life is so complex; you never know if you can trust people"), or you can speak so specifically that people may think you are keeping notes for a court case against them ("I saw you at 10:32 P.M. on Friday, January 29, at the right-hand corner table of Harry's Bar with a 6-foot, brown-haired man wearing black jeans, boots, and a powder-blue T-shirt").

As such, the use of language by one person does not necessarily call up the original image in another. Highly abstract language creates many opportunities for misinterpretation between communicators. Lower abstractions, more specific language, leaves less room for misinterpretation. Finding the appropriate level of abstraction in language use is important to competent communication.

Effective communicators should try to choose the appropriate level of abstraction. It should be higher in some circumstances and lower in others. Determining the appropriate level of abstraction involves considering yourself, your audience, and the situation.

People often use high-level abstractions to avoid the pain of specifics. For example, "I'm sorry for your loss" (high) may be more sensitive than "I'm sorry your little brown cocker spaniel was run over by the blue Nissan Pulsar" (low). The politician says, "We should guarantee the personal freedoms of every citizen" (high) to avoid offending some (and losing their votes) by saying, "I think you should be able to carry a handgun if you want" (low).

CHECKLIST

Determining the Appropriate Level of Abstraction

✓ **Consider using high-level abstraction related to your own goals.** Try high abstractions to group people or concepts together ("my classmates"), to avoid confrontation or evaluation ("I was out"), or to provide a generality that you think someone can identify with ("I've been there").

✓ **Consider the person(s) you are talking to you.** Ask yourself whether they are likely to be offended by specifics ("You put one too many garlic cloves in the sauce"), whether past encounters have led you to believe that they will listen better to high or to low abstractions, and whether they are feeling defensive (in which case you may want to avoid words that would make them more so).

✓ **Consider the situation and context.** In giving a speech, you may often use high abstractions to get people to identify with your position ("Everyone here loves freedom") and use low abstractions in the form of statistics to justify a major point ("Handguns kill 65,000 people in this country every year"). If you are talking with defensive employees, you might use high abstractions to show workers how much they are valued ("You are such great workers") but use low abstractions to give them specific instructions about how to correct specific errors ("This report will be much better if you go back and put in the subtitles I've asked for and run it through the spellchecker").

Lower level abstractions are usually clearer; they help you understand more precisely what people mean. While "Get something interesting at the video store" (high) allows a wide range of choices, saying, "I'd like to watch a mystery movie tonight" (lower) is more likely to get you something you'll appreciate. Asking for a specific movie (lower still) will ensure your satisfaction with the choice.

Some situations call for the use of both high- and low-level abstractions. Others demand a medium level of language abstraction. At still other times, your ethical sense will tell you what type of language is appropriate. The other person, the situation, and your own goals for the interaction will determine the most effective level of abstraction.

People use a wide variety of language strategies in their interpersonal relationships to define the relationship, to express the level of commitment, and to achieve influence or control over the relational partner.

THE LANGUAGE OF RELATIONSHIP DEFINITION

Language helps define relationships. For example, it is fairly easy to label your mother, father, sister, brother, aunt, uncle, grandfather, grandmother, son, daughter — your closest blood relations — as you introduce any of these people to others. If you say, "I'd like you to meet my boss, Mr. Ramiro Sanchez," you are describing the status and professional relationship that you have. The introduction sets the stage for how people are to be treated and what further communication might go on. Introducing someone as a stepbrother, however, can require more explanation than a person wants to give. So it may be preferable to introduce him as a brother, without bothering to produce the complex relational definitions. You might introduce a co-worker who has a slightly higher or lower status than you by saying, "Rosalinda and I work together," to avoid implications of superiority or inferiority.

THE LANGUAGE OF INTIMACY AND DISTANCE

Telling people about yourself and finding out about them occurs at all levels of building relationships. The more intimate the level of your relationship, the more intimate are the revelations that usually occur. Speaking about intense feelings or opinions does not normally occur in beginning relationships. Your thoughts and feelings — more intimate disclosures about self — are reserved for relationships that have a base of trust. For example, in the early stages of your relationships, language is very general. You usually do not verbally disagree with others, and you spend most of your time trying to find out things you and your partner have in common ("You like basketball? I love to watch the Pacers"). You may share a lot of biographical information, and you usually stick to "safe" topics, engaging in the small talk of not-so-intimate relationships.

As relationships become more intimate, the language of inclusion begins. "We like Chinese food" indicates that one person feels free to speak for another. This language of inclusion makes extensive use of "we" and "us" language. Talking about the other and self increases ("Leticia and I always rent videos on Friday night"). The use of pet names ("honey," "schmoopie") usually occurs, as well as sarcasm or teasing. This language of affiliation defines the relationship to those within it as well as to those outside of it. (You may at times feel embarrassed or repelled by hearing some of the intimate terms people call one another.)

Intimate relationships use language that implies future commitment ("Where shall we spend the holiday next year?"). Planning goes on, and decisions are made jointly. "Maybe in a few years we can afford a bigger house" makes use of "we" language as well as future planning. Mutual understandings guide language use. It is possible to say, "Let's get the families together for a big barbeque" because the parties assume they will be together in the future and that they have some claim on each other's future.

If people in a relationship are disengaging, they will often talk around important topics—like the status of their own relationship. They maintain a stony silence, or they fill the silences with "empty talk" or "safe talk" about topics that don't involve the relationship.

THE LANGUAGE OF CONTROL

As we have noted, interpersonal relationships work out many different ways of balancing control and influence, and language is just one of the tools communicative partners use to gain and relinquish relational controls. Asking another for favors indicates a more intimate relationship, but it is also a control move: You are trying to get the other to do something for you. Interrupting another or changing the subject of a conversation is also a control attempt. In such instances, the role of control is obvious.

The use of control is not always so obvious. Refusing to talk about something the other wants to talk about can appear to be trivial but is actually a very influential move. Cajoling, or "sweet talk," may persuade the other to do what you want even though it doesn't seem very forceful on the surface. In competent relationships, language that seems less powerful may actually contribute to the competence of the relationship. Using hesitant language with your partner may be a way of accommodating.

The language you use in an interpersonal communication setting can give clues to the intimacy of a relationship and to where the partners "stand" with one another. The language can express liking, love, and respect—or dislike, hate, and disrespect. The language can say, "Let's be best friends" or "Let's give it a rest for a while." The language can define us as friends, business partners, family, enemies, past lovers, or former neighbors. The language labels you use for your communicative partner are language clues to your interpersonal relationship, but so are the topics you discuss or don't, the depth of your conversations, and the things you don't say at all.

NONVERBAL COMMUNICATION

A variety of nonverbal behaviors accompany language—pauses, stutters, the tone and volume of the voice, the speed at which someone speaks, the accents one uses, the gestures made while speaking, and many other body movements. **Nonverbal communication** involves:

- behavior rather than the content of spoken words
- meaning attributed to that behavior

Therefore, **nonverbal communication** is the process of signaling meaning through behavior that does not involve the content of spoken words. Nonverbal communication consists of messages (intentional or unintentional) that are encoded and decoded with meaning and that serve specific functions. Because virtually every behavior can be interpreted as having meaning, you are continually communicating. A sigh, a nod, and a tapping foot can all convey meaning.

The **codes** of nonverbal communication (as with any other coding system) are the means by which messages are sent and received. Simply put, these are the types of behavior that produce potential messages. In order to better understand the meaning of a message, it is important to know the codes used in communicating messages. Nonverbal behavior can be classified into the following categories of codes: appearance and artifacts; gestures and body movements; facial expressions and eye behavior; paralanguage; touch and the use of space; time orientation; and scents and smells.

APPEARANCE AND ARTIFACTS

Whether subconsciously or deliberately, we all make judgments based on appearance. Appearance affects not only perceptions of attractiveness, but also judgments about a person's background, character, personality, status, and future behavior.[4] These perceptions are inferred from body shape and size, facial features, skin color, clothing, and **artifacts**—or accessories used for decoration or identification. Jewelry, glasses, hats, badges, tattoos, purses, and briefcases are all personal artifacts. Through your appearance and artifacts, you can nonverbally communicate your self-image, affiliation, and social attitudes.

GESTURES AND BODY MOVEMENTS

The nonverbal behavior code with which you are probably the most familiar is kinesics. Sometimes called "body language," **kinesics** refers to the way gestures and body movements send messages. There are five categories of kinesic behavior:

- **Emblems.** Emblems are movements and gestures that have a direct verbal translation and are displayed to replace words. Examples include the hitchhiker's thumb, the two-finger victory sign, and a wave of the hand to say hello.

- **Illustrators.** Illustrators accompany verbal messages and illustrate what is being said. They are usually intentional by the sender, and cannot normally be interpreted without the use of words. Holding your hands a foot apart while saying, "The fish was this big!" is an example of an illustrator.

- **Regulators.** Regulators are used to regulate conversations. Examples include raising your hand, lifting your head, or raising your eyebrows to gain the floor during a conversation.

- **Adapters.** Adapters satisfy some physical or psychological need, and are not conscious behaviors. Physical adapters include rubbing your eyes when tired and shifting positions in a chair after sitting for a long time. Psychological adapters are used for emotional release and include twisting your hair and biting your nails when you're nervous.

- **Affect displays.** Affect displays convey mood and reactions. These are usually unintentional movements that reflect the sender's true emotions. An example is slumping in a chair (indicating fatigue or boredom) or a sad face (reflecting problems in your life).

FACIAL EXPRESSIONS AND EYE BEHAVIOR

Facial expressions are the primary nonverbal codes we use to display emotions. The human face is capable of producing over 1,000 different expressions.[5] Nonetheless, different facial expressions are associated with different emotions, and these emotions are displayed by distinct areas of the face.

- *Happiness* is shown in the cheek/mouth and eye/eyelid areas.
- *Sadness* and *fear* are conveyed in the eye/eyelid area.
- *Surprise* is portrayed in the cheek/mouth, eye/eyelid, and brow/forehead areas.
- *Anger* is not easily noticeable unless two or more areas of the face are used for its expression.

The eye area is one of the least controllable regions of your face, and as a result, your eyes can expose your emotional state. **Oculesics** refers to eye behavior and plays an important role in communication.

INTERPERSONAL COMMUNICATION IN CULTURAL PERSPECTIVE

Cultural Differences in Saying Hello Nonverbally

Culture	Nonverbal Code for Hello
Japan	The bow — bending forward and down at the waist.
India	*Namaste* — placing hands at the chest in a praying position and bowing slightly.
Thailand	*Wai* — same as *namaste* (India).
Middle East	*Salaam* — used primarily among the older generation. Right hand moves upward, touching first the heart, then the forehead, and then moving up into the air.
Maori tribespeople (New Zealand) and Eskimos	Rubbing noses.
East African tribes	Spitting at each other's feet.
Tibetan tribesmen	Sticking out their tongues at each other.
Bolivia	Handshake accompanied by a hearty clap on the back.
Russia	Friends begin with a handshake and move to a "bear hug."
Latin America	*Abrazo* — embracing with both arms.

Source: Data from R. E. Axtell, *Gestures: The Do's and Taboos of Body Language around the World* (New York: John Wiley & Sons, 1991).

Eye contact with another person commands involvement. Even when you pass a stranger and make eye contact, you are connected to that person, albeit remotely. It can also stimulate arousal, either positive or negative. You can probably remember as a child receiving "looks" from your parents that communicated a specific meaning and emotion to you — eye contact that sent messages of "Be careful" or "You're in trouble when we get home." Even now, you communicate with friends in much the same way. Imagine meeting a classmate as you walk with your best friend. With eye contact, you could communicate to your friend such messages as "Can you believe that outfit?" or "Hurry, I don't want him to see me!"

From a general perspective, eye behavior can serve six important communicative functions.[6] The eyes can:

- influence attitude change and persuasion

- indicate degrees of attentiveness, interest, and arousal
- express emotions
- regulate interaction
- indicate power and status
- form impressions in others

Interpersonal encounters usually begin with eye contact to signal interest, and in Western cultures, increased eye contact with a speaker indicates interest and attention. The type and amount of eye contact can reveal the nature and stage of a relationship as well as status. If you think about it, the amount of eye contact you make with others is indicative of how much you like them.

PARALANGUAGE

Paralanguage refers to how something is said, not what is said. To illustrate this point, try saying the word "great" to convey these messages: disappointment, excitement, congratulations, and disgust. The word (what you said) didn't change, but the voice characteristics (how you said it) changed. People make judgments about personal characteristics (age, gender, status, etc.), emotional states, and attraction on the basis of vocal cues. Vocal cues also influence persuasion and aid comprehension.[7]

Paralanguage can be classified into two major categories that are closely related to achieving effective interpersonal communication.

- **Voice qualities** encompass pitch range (actual range of pitch), vocal lip control (the degree of hoarseness in a voice), glottis control (sharp or smooth transitions in pitch), articulation control (precise or slurred speech), rhythm control (level of smoothness), resonance (thickness or thinness of tone), pitch control (the ability to vary range of pitches), and tempo (rate of speed of speech).[8]

- **Vocalizations** are vocal cues outside language structure. There are three types of vocalizations: *vocal characterizers, vocal qualifiers,* and *vocal segregates. Vocal characterizers* include sounds such as laughing, crying, giggling, moaning, sighing, and yawning. Vocal characterizers give information about the speaker's emotional or physical state. *Vocal qualifiers* are cues that provide variety within a specific utterance. This category includes intensity (loudness or softness), pitch height (high or low), extent (duration of sound), and rate. For example, an uneven rhythm (shakiness in the voice) and a fast tempo (rate) might indicate nervousness, and little resonance (thinness in voice) and slurred speech (articulation control) might signal fatigue. *Vocal segregates* are used in place of words and have connotative meaning. These include "uh-huh" (yes), "shhh" (be quiet), and "uh-uh" (no). Filler sounds like "er" or "ah" are also considered segregates.

TOUCH

Tactile communication, or **haptics**, refers to touching behavior. Touch is one of the most fundamental types of communication. Touch is powerful communication and provides meaning when words often fail. A father's loving touch soothes a crying baby; a handshake thanks a public speaker; a supportive pat on the back bolsters the confidence of the unsure. Although people have different perceptions of touch and some are more accepting of it than others, it is a primary means of communication and fulfills a basic human need.

Touching can communicate a variety of messages. Although not all people interpret touch in the same way, it allows people to communicate emotion—and the intensity of that emotion—more effectively.

SPACE

Proxemics refers to how you use and communicate with space. One area of proxemics is personal space, the space around your body to which you attach ownership. Cultural norms and personal feelings about space will affect your choices about the use of this space.

Hall devised a system of identification for the space used, or spatial zones, based on the type of interpersonal relationship.[9] Hall categorizes spatial zones as

- **Intimate (0–18 inches).** This zone is reserved for lovers, very close friends, and family members.
- **Personal (18 inches–4 feet).** This zone is used for close friends and relatives.
- **Social (4–12 feet).** This zone is used for professional interactions, such as business transactions or teacher–student conferences and for casual talks.
- **Public (12 feet and beyond).** This zone is used for keeping distance between the interactants, such as concert performers with their audience.

Your personal space needs may vary from these general guidelines, but how you feel about allowing another person to be in one of your spaces really depends on who that other person is. Some families are close and use intimate and personal zones exclusively; other families are uncomfortable with that much closeness. Different cultures around the world vary a great deal in their preferences for proxemic closeness. Arab cultures, for example, encourage very close proxemics so that sight, smell, and touch are heightened for communicators.

TIME ORIENTATION

Chronemics refers to how people perceive and structure time. **Time orientations** fall into three categories:

- **Psychological.** Psychological time orientation is the way you perceive or feel about time. *Past-oriented people* assign particular value to past events; *present-oriented people* live and work for the present; and *future-oriented people* live and work for the future. A person's orientation will determine the importance that person ascribes to conversation content, the length of the interaction, the urgency of the interaction, and punctuality.[10]

- **Biological.** Biological time orientation is determined by biological cycles. This is your "biological clock." It determines when you are most active, both physically and mentally. Biological time affects how you perceive others and how they perceive you and can thus be a source of communication problems. An early-morning person will perceive a late-night person's level of attention in the morning negatively, whereas the late-night person will perceive the early-morning person's tiredness in the afternoon in an unfavorable way.

- **Cultural.** Cultural time orientation is the way a culture uses time. For example, most Western cultures find it extremely rude to be late, but in most Latin cultures lateness is the norm. The phrase "time is money," used extensively in Western cultures, indicates how people in those cultures value time.

SCENTS AND SMELLS

The perception of scents and smells is referred to as **olfactics**. Scents and smells can produce strong reactions and can add intensity to positive or negative perceptions. Consider how bleach stings the eyes and forces people to retreat from the odor. Consider, too, how the aroma of fresh-baked bread brings a pleasant smile. In much the same way, personal scents and smells affect interactions. Offensive odors will increase the distance between interactants and shorten the time of the interaction. Pleasant smells will increase communication with another.[11] Body scents and smells in the environment communicate things to us about others. Our judgments about other people may be influenced by the odors those people allow in their environment.

Nonverbal communication affects every interaction, every relationship, and every dimension of your life. It can destroy careers (e.g., when a businessperson touches a colleague inappropriately), elevate relationships (e.g., when congratulations are expressed by a handshake or a pat on the back), or determine future interactions (e.g., when an appropriate greeting is used in a foreign culture). As an effective interpersonal communicator, you must remain aware of how nonverbal communication manages relationships, controls interactions, persuades, deceives, and forms impressions. You should take into consideration all the variables that can modify the message: culture, context, situation, and the relational dimension.

One ingredient not mentioned previously is as much a part of nonverbal communication as any other factor—individuality. Nonverbal behavior is not always transmitted by the same channels, received with the intended message, or sent with explicit meaning. Individuals differ in the codes they use, how they use them, and the messages they apply to them. The variety of messages and ways to communicate those messages are infinite. That is one of the fascinating aspects of nonverbal communication. Individual differences, preferences, and variations of behavior should be enjoyed. An appreciation of nonverbal behaviors that are culturally different from our own enriches our communication experience and enhances our effectiveness as interpersonal communicators as we begin to recognize the importance of individual expression.

LISTENING

Listening is the process of recognizing, understanding, and accurately interpreting the messages communicated by others. Effective listening as an interpersonal communicator involves a complex process of cognitive, behavioral, and affective skills.

Listening needs vary. You don't listen the same way in every situation; rather, you listen according to your needs. There are four major types of listening:[12]

- **Comprehensive Listening.** The type of listening used to understand the message of another person is comprehensive listening. You use comprehensive listening in class as you try to understand what the instructor is presenting. A person giving you directions, someone providing instructions, or an individual recounting an experience all require comprehensive listening.

- **Empathic Listening.** Listening to people with openness, sensitivity, and caring constitutes empathic listening. If you listen with empathy, you are attempting to know how the other person feels at the time. Empathic listening can serve to comfort a person when disaster or disappointment has struck, as when you are sensitive to a friend's story of a failing grade. People in love engage in empathic listening when they are exchanging deep thoughts about their relationship. They want each other to understand the feelings involved.

- **Critical Listening.** When you listen in order to evaluate or analyze information, evidence, ideas, or opinions, you are engaged in critical listening. Critical listening involves making a judgment about the nature of a message. You may hear something on television that you find difficult to believe, or you may listen to a political speaker on the radio and suspect that the person is just trying to win votes. These are examples of critical listening. You may even find classroom material to be suspicious. If you listen with an evaluative posture, you are listening critically.

- **Appreciative Listening.** Appreciative listening is used when your goal is simply to appreciate the sounds that your listening mechanism receives. Listening to music, poetry, narrations, comedy routines, plays, movies,

CHECKLIST

Strategies for Applying the Four Functions of Listening

Comprehensive Listening

✓ Listen for main ideas or details.

✓ Listen for organizational patterns.

✓ Take the speaker's perspective.

✓ Use memory effectively.

Empathic Listening

✓ Focus on the speaker's perspective.

✓ Give supportive and understanding feedback.

✓ Show caring.

✓ Demonstrate patience.

✓ Avoid judgment.

✓ Focus on the speaker's goal.

Critical Listening

✓ Determine the speaker's goal.

✓ Evaluate the source of the message.

✓ Question the logic, reasoning, and evidence of the message.

Appreciative Listening

✓ Remove physical and time distractions.

✓ Know more about the source (for example, the artist, composer, or speaker).

✓ Explore new appreciative listening opportunities.

or television shows for sheer enjoyment would qualify as appreciative listening situations.

Listening is more than just hearing. Hearing is an audiological sequence that involves mostly involuntary physiological processes, much like breathing or the senses of sight and smell. Your capacity for hearing is only part of your ability to listen. There are many audible sounds that you hear, but listening to them is a different story. The point is, you must have good hearing to listen effectively, but hearing is only the beginning of the process.

The good news about listening is that it is a skill that can be improved. Now that you have made the commitment to improve your listening, here is a framework that will help you. This framework involves a five-step process leading to the goal of competent listening:

- The first step toward competent listening is **managing your listening skills**. First, assess your listening self-concept. Next, determine your actual listening efficiency. Listening tests can give you an idea of your strengths and weaknesses. This leads to an assessment of listening barriers. Are you bored, anxious, or defensive when some people speak? Understanding goal-setting completes Step 1 of this process.

- Step 2 in this process is **managing the listening context**. The listening context includes the setting, cultural factors, and third parties. The setting is a composite of place, emotion, and time. All of these factors have their own influence on the listening context. Cultural factors are important as well. Being sensitive to and respecting one another's cultural background are prerequisites for competent listening. Third parties influence a listening situation. Sometimes this is an advantage. In other instances, third-party influences may hinder your listening and you must take steps to avoid any distractions they create.

- Step 3 involves **adjusting to the speaker**. Relational history and a speaker's expectations are important elements. Because many speakers do not adjust to their listeners, it is your job as a listener to adjust to them as best you can. Understanding a speaker's communication style involves accurately interpreting vocal characteristics, remaining objective about a speaker's word choice, and understanding how a speaker's style can form particular impressions on you as a listener.

- **Listening critically** is Step 4 in this framework. To listen critically, first you must determine the main point of the message. Next, you must focus your efforts on the listening task. Besides its importance in decoding the verbal message, critical listening requires recognizing and understanding the speaker's nonverbal cues. In order to use the information communicated by the speaker, you must also use your memory effectively.

- Step 5, **listening interactively**, involves facilitating the speaker's communication so that his or her messages are easier for you to understand.

One way to help speakers understand your level of listening competency is to provide appropriate nonverbal cues. Verbal reinforcers can let the speaker know that the listener agrees, understands, or is confused by the message. Questions will keep the speaker on track or provide clarification or verification of information in the message.

3 Developing and Maintaining Interpersonal Relationships

Relationships play a central role in determining the type of communication that is most effective and appropriate. In turn, competent interpersonal communication permits more meaningful relationships to develop. Each of you is involved in a number of relationships of different levels of importance. No one can offer you a guaranteed plan for a perfect relationship. However, by understanding how relationships form and disengage and what components make up a relationship, you may better understand your own relationships.

THE ROLE OF RELATIONSHIPS IN INTERPERSONAL COMMUNICATION

A **relationship** is the interconnection or interdependence of two (or more) people in order to achieve some goal. A **communication relationship** is one in which the interdependence is based on symbolic exchange. If this definition

CHECKLIST

Thinking about Your Own Experiences with Interpersonal Communication

As you begin to explore interpersonal communication, ask yourself these questions about your experiences in communicating interpersonally:

✓ Why do some relationships fail while others intensify? How can we improve our current relationships by applying communication theories?

✓ How do I decide to initiate an interpersonal relationship? What should I not talk about in the initiation phase of a relationship?

✓ From your own experience, provide an example of a productive conflict and a destructive conflict. What factors contributed to making these situations productive or destructive?

✓ How do the dynamics of a relationship change when people of different cultures are involved? How can issues of language, eye contact, touch, worldviews, and values affect an intercultural relationship?

✓ What ethical issues should I consider in interpersonal relationships?

leads you to think that you begin and end several communication relationships each day, you are correct. But since minimal relationships (those that last only momentarily and have little consequence for you) are usually not very interesting, we will confine our discussion to relationships that are meaningful for the participants over a period of time.

THE ROLE OF THE INDIVIDUAL

Individuals embark on relationships with their self-concepts, personal experiences, preferred styles of communicating and thinking (cognitive processing), individual goals, and the like. All of these characteristics profoundly influence how they will communicate in any given conversation or relationship.

Although individuals are not lost in relationships, the influence of their partners usually leads to changes in the participants. The more important the relationship, the more influence the individuals will have on their partners and, thus, the more susceptible each is to change. This is especially the case if the participants in the relationship like each other or if one has a lot of status or desirable qualities in the eyes of the other(s). As romantic partners become more involved and committed, for example, they usually adapt to one another, taking on similar habits, mannerisms, and attitudes. This adaptation is a consequence of the influence or control the partners have over each other. A manager may have a similar effect on employees, with the employees coming to see the business world — and talk about it — in much the same way as the boss does. In hostile relationships, the partners may change in ways that make them more distinct from each other.

THE ROLE OF RELATIONAL KNOWLEDGE

Relational knowledge is the information you gain through your experiences in relationships. This knowledge greatly influences your behavior, communication style, perceptions, and self-concept. As your relationships grow and develop, you begin to form theories about how others will act, feel, and think in response to your actions. These hypotheses are referred to as *schemas*, and they guide your processing of information.

Relational schemas are the bits and pieces of information that you use to interpret the messages you receive in a relationship.[1] Jay has never had a serious girlfriend and considers himself unlucky in love. For example, whenever Jay has attempted a serious relationship, he has been told that he is immature, insensitive, and incapable of maintaining an adult relationship. Jay and Lesley have gone out a few times, but Jay will not pursue a serious relationship with Lesley because he fears rejection. Jay's previous experiences have formed a schema that stops him from initiating any serious relationship.

Relational history also plays an important role in relational knowledge. Relational history is the set of thoughts, perceptions, and impressions you have formed about current or previous relational partners. If you hold positive views about a former partner and later run into that person again, you will react differently than if your history were more negative. For example, Isabella has always focused on what she wants in life. She has worked in the county hospital since her volunteering days during high school and has become very knowledgeable in her field. Louise, the head nurse in pediatrics, first met Isabella as a candy striper and knows that Isabella recently obtained an LVN (licensed vocational nurse) degree. Louise's relational history of Isabella helped Louise nominate Isabella for the RN (registered nurse) college scholarship.

GOALS AND MOTIVATIONS FOR RELATIONSHIP DEVELOPMENT

Why do you enter into relationships with certain individuals and not with others? The goals and motivations behind the initiation and development of relationships vary. Expectations play a big role in why you enter into relationships, why you have relationships with certain people, and why some relationships continue to develop while others do not. However, there are yet other influences that lead you to form relationships.

INTERPERSONAL ATTRACTION

It is not always easy to explain why some people are attracted to others. Two people might be attracted to the same individual for completely different reasons. For instance, Jeremy and Connie both met Shellee at a community Fourth of July picnic. Both were attracted to her because of a "special quality" they saw in her. To Jeremy, Shellee was special because she had lived in Colón, Panama, where he had grown up. In contrast, the special quality that Connie admired was Shellee's satirical sense of humor.

Physical attractiveness is a special kind of interpersonal attraction. Western society places great emphasis on having a pleasant physical appearance. Of course, looks aren't everything, but they do play an important role in attracting others, especially in the early stages of a relationship.

PHYSICAL PROXIMITY

Long-distance relationships are difficult to maintain simply because of lack of proximity. Although some would argue that "absence makes the heart grow fonder," it can also be said, "out of sight, out of mind." Julie and Moya had a relationship that seemed very successful. They were good friends and had many similar interests. Yet when Moya moved away, the relationship quickly diminished. At first, the two spoke almost every day, but after a few weeks they spoke less frequently. Eventually, they spoke only once in a while. As often happens, each made new friends and entered new relationships. This story is possible in all types of relationships: friendships, work relationships, and romantic relationships. People who have frequent contact are more likely to develop and maintain a relationship than are those who see one another less regularly. Think about people with whom you have primarily "electronic" contact such as e-mail or instant messaging. Does this type of communication maintain your relationship even when you have infrequent personal contact?

ALLEVIATING LONELINESS

Humans feel a natural need for companionship, so it is only natural that when people are lonely, they seek out relationships with other people. A person who feels lonely tends to see a relationship as a logical answer to the problem. A relationship can act as a security blanket, helping to ward off the chill of loneliness.

STIMULATION

People have an innate need for stimulation, and the interaction between two people provides a unique kind of stimulation on a personal level. This stimulation is intellectual as well as emotional and physical.

Intellectual stimulation stems from conversations about topics of shared interest, especially current events, movies, books, and societal issues. Such conversations help people explore issues and formulate their opinions about them. Because people have emotions, they also feel a need for **emotional stimulation**. The bond created between two people in a relationship provides an opportunity for them to express their emotions. **Physical stimulation** arises from the human need to touch and be touched. You probably know people who touch while they talk or kiss and hug hello and good-bye after every encounter. Physical stimulation can be a pleasurable, healthy, and natural part of relationships—as long as it does not interfere with other relational goals.

ACHIEVING GOALS

Some people enter into relationships to achieve certain goals. For example, if you have dreamed all your life about doing public service work overseas, you might seek relationships with influential people in that field. Similarly, if you are looking to advance your career, you might try to develop relationships with your superiors and co-workers. Often, your initial motivation for developing a relationship with a particular individual is to see what that person can do for you or how he or she can help you. Of course, the other person will have goals that may or may not be compatible with your own. Therefore, the negotiation of mutual or compatible goals is an important process in relationships.

TYPES OF RELATIONSHIPS

There are as many different types of relationships as there are individuals who make up these relationships. Some common relationships are those between co-workers, between doctors and patients, and between salespeople and clients. However, we will focus our attention on the two most important types of relationships: friendship and family.

FRIENDSHIP

Friendship is a relationship between two or more people that is perceived as mutually satisfying, productive, and beneficial.

Characteristics of Friendship

Everyone has a personal opinion on what important qualities a friend should have, but six general characteristics of a friend include:[2]

- **Availability.** If the parties in a relationship seldom interact with each other, the relationship often deteriorates or loses its closeness. What good would a friend be who was never available to spend time with you? People want friends to make time for them and be accessible.

- **Caring.** You want your friends to care about you. Even if something in your life is of little importance to them, you want and expect them to care about what happens because it's important to you. Your friends do not have to agree with the choices or events in your life, but they need to care about them. An individual who ignores you, has no regard for your feelings, and seems not to care about what happens will not be identified as a friend.

- **Honesty.** Honesty is a virtue that is vital in all relationships. You want your friends to be open and honest with you. When a relational partner deceives you, the deception tends to decrease the degree of closeness that the two of you shared. Sometimes your friends may have to be "brutally honest" and tell you things that you would rather not hear. You have to accept this honesty as constructive criticism and remember that, although you may not like what you are hearing, you may need to hear it and hearing it from a friend may actually be best.

- **Confidentiality.** You want confidentiality from your friends. In other words, you want to be sure that what you disclose to your friends will not end up in the local newspaper tomorrow. You want to be able to trust your friends and know that they will not share your deepest, darkest secrets with others.

- **Loyalty.** A friend who can be loyal in even the worst of times is a lifelong friend. A true friend is one who is loyal and would never allow others to degrade you without standing up for you or at least letting it be known that he or she did not agree with what was being said.

- **Empathy.** Empathy is the understanding one has of another's experience. You want your friends to be able to see particular circumstances as you do and perhaps walk in your shoes. Even if they have never shared the same experiences, you expect friends to try to empathize with you.

Types of Friendship

Even though the six characteristics we have discussed may seem to apply to all friendships, it is important to understand that there are different types of friendship. Communication researcher John Reisman has identified three types:[3]

- **Reciprocity.** Reciprocity is a type of friendship that is composed of characteristics such as self-surrender, loyalty, mutual respect, affection, and support. Each individual in a reciprocal friendship equally gives and takes, and each person shares the responsibility of maintaining the relationship. For example, Antwaan and Russell are friends who help one another in any way they can, and they find spending time with one another to be enjoyable and beneficial. They feel they can trust one another, and they are always comfortable when they are together. Clearly, Antwaan and Russell's friendship is one of reciprocity.

- **Receptivity.** In receptive friendships, there is an imbalance between the giving and taking, with one partner being the primary giver and the other the primary taker. However, this is not always a bad arrangement. The needs of each person can be met through the particular roles played. This type of friendship often develops between individuals of different status. For example, Ramon is a teaching assistant for a class that Elise is taking. Elise is on the volleyball team, and traveling causes her to miss several classes. Elise must meet with Ramon every time she misses a class to get the information she needs, and through their frequent meetings the two have become friends. Elise is using Ramon's access to information, and although Ramon is not receiving anything comparable from Elise in return, they still value each other's friendship.

- **Association.** Association can be seen as a relationship with an acquaintance rather than as a true friendship. An associative friendship is most likely to develop between people who have frequent contact, such as co-workers, classmates, or neighbors. For example, Holly and Susan are in three classes together, and throughout the semester the two have become friends. Even though they do not do anything together outside class, they still consider each other friends.

FAMILY

Whether it's your immediate family or perhaps a more extended family, you have relational and blood ties to other people whom you call **family** — "a social group having specified roles and statuses (e.g., husband, wife, father, mother, son, daughter) with ties of blood, marriage, or adoption who usually share a common residence and cooperate economically."[4] Healthy families strive for effective communication in ensuring mental, intellectual, and emotional growth; promoting family ties; and helping each other to succeed in their goals. It is through communication that families generate their strengths.

CHECKLIST

Improving Family Relations

Just about every family could improve the relationships among its members. Here are several recommendations that will help enrich family relationships through competent communication.

- **Put yourself in their place.** To understand what family members are feeling, you must show some degree of empathy, not just sympathy. Try to grasp how they feel, even if your own experiences are different.

- **Let others know how you feel.** Family members must be able to tell or show one another how they are feeling. If one member is angry about something that happened at school, the others will not know what is wrong unless they are told. If a hurt individual keeps feelings to him- or herself and acts upset, others may perceive that this anger is directed toward something they did.

- **Be flexible.** As each member grows and develops, so will the relationships with others. For example, a daughter in a family may be extremely close to her father at the age of ten, but at the age of sixteen she may become significantly closer to her mother. The parents must recognize this change as normal and must not see it as a failing on their part.

- **Fight fairly.** Listen to the other person and attempt to understand the other person's point of view. Do not "hit below the belt" or gang up on one another. Compromise is extremely important, and there does not always have to be a definite winner and loser.

- **Give as much as you take.** All family members have times when they are allowed to take more than they give, but there are also times when they must give more than they take. Remember, how would you like it if other family members made excessive demands on you?

Functions of Families

The family fulfills needs such as food, shelter, clothing, and basic caretaking. At the time of birth, a human infant is unable to care for him- or herself; a family is needed to ensure the infant's survival. Without the family, infants and most young children would be helpless. Older family members also require care. As more people live longer, their need for daily care increases. Whether older adults live within the household of an offspring, as in an extended family, or live elsewhere, their care usually falls to the family.

The family helps us discover what is appropriate behavior. Long before children enter school, they begin to learn important basic lessons. Many of the beliefs and values you hold are shaped and influenced by your family through a process of observation and cultivation. Younger family members watch parents and older siblings as they interact with others in various contexts, learning how to handle themselves and other people in social situations. Family members encourage social skills in younger children through instructive and corrective communication practices.

Family members interact with one another in different recreational contexts. Many families engage in activities that they enjoy doing together. Sports, working in the yard, or just lounging together on a lazy Sunday afternoon provide recreational opportunities for family members. Finally, recreational time can greatly influence the closeness of the family.

The family is the medium through which family customs or basic cultural guidelines can be passed from one generation to the next. Children tend to imitate their parents and other family members; many children will arrange their homes like the one they grew up in, buy the same brands their parents did, or even vote for the same political candidates. When family members tell stories about their parents, grandparents, and great grandparents, younger members get a sense of history and pride about the family lineage and want to help perpetuate family strength. In this way, transmission becomes an important communication function for many families.

STAGES OF RELATIONSHIPS

Although each relationship is unique, relationships can go through six possible stages of relational development:

- Initiation
- Exploration
- Intensification
- Stablization
- Decline
- Termination

It is important to note that not all relationships experience each of these stages, particularly the last two, decline and termination. Assume that all relationships start with an initial stage. Many will proceed to an exploratory phase; some of these relationships will go on to intensification, and some of those will become stable. If at any point in the process costs exceed rewards, relational decline may result. If relational partners are willing to work at the relationship, repair strategies may be attempted, moving the relationship back to one of its previous stages. If relational decline has reached a "point of no return," termination strategies may be used to exit the relationship altogether.[5]

THE INITIATION STAGE

When you begin or *initiate* a relationship, you are probably uncertain about your potential partner. Your expectations and knowledge are based on general information gained from the partner's appearance, demeanor, and behavior. After some contact with the person, you may begin to form impressions that confirm or modify your knowledge, expectations, and motives for being in the relationship. Positive impressions (assessments) translate into rewards, whereas negative impressions are perceived as costs. If costs seem to outweigh rewards, the relationship will probably end at this point. If enough rewards are present, the relationship will move to the exploratory stage.

THE EXPLORATION STAGE

The exploratory stage consists primarily of information seeking. It assumes that both relational partners want to reduce uncertainty. In the exploratory stage, relational partners are hesitant to delve into highly intimate topics, as they are still testing the relationship. As information is exchanged, expectations, knowledge, and motives are reassessed, and rewards and costs are reexamined. If costs exceed rewards, relational decline is likely; if rewards are abundant, the next stage further intensifies the relationship.

THE INTENSIFICATION STAGE

By the time relational partners reach this stage, they have made an investment in each other and can afford to intensify their relationship. Instead of seeking personal information about each other, the partners are more likely to focus on the relationship. Intensification reflects a desire to move the relationship to a new level. Both relational partners realize that their expectations, motives, and knowledge are different from those in the earlier stages, so they assess rewards and costs along new lines. For example, two friends who are intensifying their relationship will know not to hold unrealistic expectations because their relational knowledge has grown. They may even develop new motives for being in the relationship. In the earlier stages, they may have valued companionship, but now they value their partner's trust more than anything else. It is in the intensification stage that relational intimacy or closeness may be felt for the first time.

THE STABILIZATION STAGE

By the time relational partners have reached this stable stage, their relationship is no longer volatile or temporary, they have a great deal of knowledge about one another, their expectations are accurate and realistic, and they feel comfortable with their motives for being in the relationship. Perceptions of rewards and costs become more stable, providing a measure of predictability in the relationship. This is not to say that relationships don't continue to evolve, for in order for relationships to enjoy stability, they must continue to interest the partners.

Communication researcher W. Wilmot characterizes stable relationships in the following three ways:[6]

CHECKLIST

Paths to Stable Relationships

Maintaining successful relationships requires a great deal of effort. You can try to achieve stable relationships by adopting the following behaviors.

✓ **Be understanding.** Try to understand how your partner views the world. Empathize with his or her fears, pain, and dreams. Do not judge these concerns. Aim only to understand in order to communicate more effectively with your partner. Show that you care.

✓ **Reveal your feelings.** Self-disclosure is an essential part of a relationship. It strengthens the bond between relational partners. Be careful, though, to use good judgment and to reveal yourself cautiously. It may be detrimental to self-disclose too much. Knowledge of past acts or feelings may harm the relationship if disclosed at the wrong time.

✓ **Be flexible.** Recognize that people and relationships naturally change. Often, conscious change is necessary on the part of one or both of the relational partners.

✓ **Be accommodating.** Conflict naturally occurs. Proceed with the goal of reaching a compromise instead of winning the argument; otherwise, one or both partners may get hurt. Conflict can be healthy, but when approached incorrectly it can be very detrimental.

✓ **Don't demand too much.** Be realistic in your expectations of your partner and of the relationship. Since most relationships experience similar kinds of trouble, do not compare your relationship with other relationships that you perceive to be better than your own.

- Relationships stabilize because the participants reach some minimal agreement on what they want from the relationship.
- Relationships can stabilize at differing levels of intimacy.
- A stabilized relationship still has areas of change occurring in it.

Intimacy and Love

Intimacy is a special aspect of relational development that is found in the stable phase.[7] **Intimacy** is a deep understanding of another person and is one of the highest levels that a relationship can aspire to. One popular misconception about intimacy is that it is usually sexual. On the contrary, intimacy is not restricted to romantic relationships. As noted earlier, it can occur between parent and child, best friends, and colleagues; even adversaries can enjoy intimacy if they have a deep understanding of one another.

Intimacy is unique in each relationship, and how you and your partner sustain intimacy is also unique. No matter which strategies you use, you should remember that an intimate relationship requires continuous maintenance.

Love expresses a wide range of feelings, from deep passion for another person to great fondness for a favorite dessert. Saying "I love you" seems to have lost some of its emphasis and does not appear to have the definite meaning it once did.

Love generally involves an exclusive, stable kind of relationship. The relationship of people who claim to be "in love" is supposed to be different from

CHECKLIST

Strategies for Maintaining Intimacy

✓ **Reciprocal self-disclosure and trust.** When individuals think that they can completely trust their partners and their partners have complete trust in them, they are more likely to self-disclose private and personal matters and create a greater sense of intimacy.

✓ **Supportive interchanges.** If you feel confident that your partner supports you 100 percent, you are likely to feel greater intimacy. To foster such interchanges, give frequent approval of your partner's activities, and avoid expressing disapproval.[8]

✓ **Commitment talk.** Relationships sustain intimacy when the partners feel an involvement and use commitment talk. Such talk could include rejection of competitors, a willingness to resolve problems, and an acceptance of personal responsibility for the relationship.[9]

✓ **Enchantment.** In the beginning, relationships are exciting and full of surprises. Later, this newness can wear off and leave the partners feeling as though every day were the same. To help maintain intimacy, partners can be enchanting, playful, mysterious, or unpredictable.

CHECKLIST

Strategies for Establishing Effective Love Relationships

No map of the road of love has ever been prepared; only trial and error, along with the passing of time and experience, will help you in your love relationships. Nonetheless, Goss and O'Hair give several helpful hints on how you may establish effective love.

✓ Develop insight into and empathy for a partner's concept of love.

✓ Analyze your own and your partner's expectations of love.

✓ Accept the fact that, even though two people have different concepts of love, neither owns the truth.

✓ Be flexible. Adapt the way you show love to meet a partner's image of loving behavior.

✓ Recall what you said or did to show loving feelings in the early stages of the relationship.

✓ Notice what your partner does to make you feel loved.

Source: B. Goss and D. O'Hair, *Communicating in Interpersonal Relationships* (New York: Macmillan, 1988).

any other relationship either might have. **Love** has been described as a permanent relationship with deep emotional ties—one that is passionate and intense.

THE DECLINE STAGE

Relationship decline, the erosion that occurs over time to some relationships, has several causes. Although no two relationships are the same, the causes of relationship decline share some similarities. Relational decline results when costs exceed rewards and relational partners put less effort into the relationship. Three factors in the costs/rewards evaluation typically lead to relational decline:

- **Uncertainty events.** Uncertainty events are events or behavioral patterns that cause uncertainty in a relationship and leave one or both partners wondering about the cause of the events and their significance for the relationship. Several factors can cause uncertainty in a relationship, including competing relationships (either dating relationships or platonic ones), an unexplained loss of closeness, a change in sexual behavior, deception or betrayal of confidence, or an unexplained change in personality or values.[10] These events or changes may be sudden and very noticeable, or they may be subtle and escape immediate attention.

- **Unmet expectations.** The way two people interact is greatly influenced by their expectations for the relationship and their perceptions of each other's expectations. These expectations range from where the relationship is going in general to very specific expectations about how the other person will react to a certain situation. Dissatisfaction with a relationship often begins when a gap forms between a person's expectations about a relationship and the actual course the relationship is taking. This is often the result of differences between the partners' respective expectations. For example, Susannah and Jiro were friends for 2 years while they were business majors at the same university. Upon graduation, Susannah went to work at a stock brokerage. When another job opened at the firm, Jiro expressed interest in it to Susannah. Although she encouraged Jiro to apply, Susannah felt uneasy mixing friendship and work and did not recommend Jiro for the position. Jiro expected Susannah, as a friend, to help him get the job. When she went against Jiro's expectations, he decided to end their friendship.

- **Interference.** Many obstacles may crop up in a relationship, interfering with its growth. Timing, third-party relationships, the family or friends of one partner, and problems with work or money can all contribute to the decline of a relationship.

THE TERMINATION STAGE

Every relationship is influenced by unique situations and circumstances, but it is still possible to make some generalizations about why relationships terminate or end. Communication researcher M. S. Davis identifies two general reasons for terminating relationships: passing away and sudden death.[11]

- **Passing away.** This reason for relationship termination is characterized by the gradual fading of the relationship. The relationship loses its vitality, and the time available for interaction may have decreased. As a result, communication and intimacy may have declined, leading to a separation of attitudes between the partners. A relationship may also pass away because the partners simply do not continue making the effort needed to maintain an intimate relationship. This leads to a stagnant relationship and a decrease in communication.

- **Sudden death.** This reason for relationship termination describes an unexpected ending that comes suddenly. Here the partners may terminate a relationship that one or both of them have desired to end for some time. Feelings that were once present may have died. Nonetheless, the partners may have continued the relationship because of circumstances external to the relationship, such as the years invested together or the presence of children.

TABLE 3.1 Strategies for Terminating a Relationship	STRATEGY	TACTICS	EXAMPLE
	Positive-tone messages	Fairness	"It wouldn't be right to go on acting like we're in love when I know I am not!"
		Compromise	"I still care about you. We can still see each other occasionally."
		Fatalism	"Destiny would never let us go on for very long in this relationship."
	Deescalation	Promise of friendship	"We can still be friends."
		Implied possible reconciliation	"We need time alone; maybe that will rekindle our feelings for each other."
		Blaming relationship	"It's not your fault, but this relationship is bogging us down."
		Appeal to independence	"We don't need to be tied down right now."
	Withdrawal/ avoidance	Avoid contact with the person as much as possible.	"I don't think I'll be able to see you this weekend."
	Justification	Emphasize positive consequences of disengaging	"It's better for you and me to see other people since we've changed so much."
		Emphasize negative consequences of not disengaging	"We will miss too many opportunities if we don't see other people."
	Negative identity management	Emphasize enjoyment of life	"Life is too short to spend with just one person right now."
		Nonnegotiation	"I need to see other people period!"

Source: Adapted from Daniel J. Canary, Michael J. Cody, and Valerie Manusov, *Interpersonal Communication: A Goals-Based Approach,* 3d ed., New York: Bedford/St. Martin's, Chapter 11.

The circumstances present in each relationship are different; accordingly, termination strategies also vary. Several common methods of terminating romantic relationships are listed in Table 3.1. Which of these strategies have worked for you in the past? How could you use some of these strategies more effectively in the future?

Effects of Termination

The termination of serious or lengthy relationships can be both traumatic and stressful. Communication researchers Harvey, Orbuch, and Weber have devised a model of termination that focuses on three effects:

- psychological needs
- communication
- posttermination mental health[12]

According to this model, after a traumatic experience, individuals experience a natural need to explain fully what happened. Months or even years may be needed to complete this process because so much information, so many details, and so much potential for second-guessing have built up. This accounting process consists of forming a detailed, coherent story about the relationship, what happened, when, why, and with what consequences. In addition, emotional consequences must be dealt with when a relationship is terminated. Both partners will experience some type of emotion in regard to the ending of their relationship. Feelings of distress, unhappiness, and disappointment are common. The relational partner who initiated the breakup may experience guilt, while the other partner may feel angry and depressed.

Reconciliation

Reconciliation is a repair strategy that goes the extra mile. It signals that one relational partner wants to rekindle an extinguished relationship. Reconciling a relationship entails a lot of risk because the other person may have no interest in a "second chance." Nonetheless, some people will launch headfirst into a series of strategies designed to rejuvenate a relationship. Other people may carefully consider the options available and construct a message that will appeal to an ex-partner.

Relationships that are begun anew may turn out in several different ways. The relationship may be strengthened by the termination and subsequent reconciliation. In this case, the partners are sure of their goals for the relationship and their feelings about each other. In other cases, old issues may not be settled and may resurface, causing the same troubles or resulting in intensified disagreement and strife. There is no way to say with any certainty how a reconciliation attempt will turn out.

EXPECTATIONS OF RELATIONSHIP DEVELOPMENT

Expectations play a central role in forming the proper interpersonal messages in relationships. Whenever people enter into a relationship, they form ideas as to what they think will or should happen. As the relationship develops, these ideas will change and some new ideas may form. Expectations have a way of influencing how people act and feel toward others. You may form expectations not only about the individual with whom you have a relationship but also about the relationship itself.

EXPECTATIONS ABOUT RELATIONSHIPS

Many people have idealistic notions about relationships. Even before relationships begin, you form expectations about future partners. Friends, families, novels, movies, and the media offer many models for you to choose from. Some people may prefer relationships that are intense but last only a short period of time, whereas others prefer intellectual, long-lasting relationships.

EXPECTATIONS ABOUT RELATIONAL PARTNERS

When people meet for the first time, they form expectations about each other, as David and Anthony did, in the following example:

DAVID: When I first met Anthony, I thought he seemed a little conservative and straitlaced. He acted as if going out and having a good time were against the law. He seemed to think that I was wild and out of control. Little did I know that we would become best friends just a short time later.

ANTHONY: I thought David was a real jerk the first time I met him. He seemed so full of himself and acted as if his only goal in life was to go out and get drunk every night. I never would have believed it if someone had told me that we would become friends.

Unrealistic Expectations

Unrealistic expectations can create problems in a relationship. Unrealistic expectations may arise because of what society says is important in a relationship. Society can give the impression that in a "good" relationship conflict will not arise. In addition, unrealistic expectations produce a great deal of unnecessary stress because such expectations are hardly ever met. As a result, people sometimes dismiss relationships that might have ultimately been beneficial.

Realistic Expectations

Realistic expectations can help prevent the development of potentially unsuccessful relationships. Yasar has a strong Muslim background and considers religion an important part of his life. Rachel is Jewish and has had very little exposure to the Muslim religion. The two are considering dating, but Yasar thinks that their religious differences are too great to overcome. He feels that Rachel will never be able to meet his expectations concerning religion. Yasar's expectations have prevented him from entering into a relationship that would probably not succeed.

Violated Expectations

The more important a relationship or individual is to you, the more you will allow violations. You may think that maintaining a relationship with an individual is more important than having your expectations met, or perhaps you may alter your expectations. Many people enter into relationships expecting a fairy-tale ending, but they soon realize that life seldom follows that kind of story line. To continue a relationship, then, you generally have to revise your expectations. Or, you may discover that the relationship or person is less important than your expectations.

The following story shows what can happen when one person in a relationship does not adhere to the expectations of the other. Roberto and Carol had been dating for two months, seeing each other every Friday and Saturday night and on Wednesday afternoons. Although they had occasionally discussed dating each other exclusively, they had not made a formal agreement to that effect. Roberto went out of town for several days and told Carol that he did not expect to return until after the weekend. But Roberto finished his trip early and arrived back in town on Friday night. On his way home, he decided to go by Carol's house to ask her out for Saturday night. He was stunned to learn that Carol was entertaining another man at her house. Roberto had formed certain expectations about his relationship with Carol, and now those expectations had, in essence, been violated. He was hurt and sad that Carol would "cheat on him."

Was Carol wrong to violate Roberto's expectations? What do you do if things do not turn out as you had hoped they would? Why are some people willing to ignore some expectancy violations, whereas others deal with unmet expectations severely? The difference probably has to do with the kind of relationship and the individuals involved.

KNOWLEDGE, MOTIVES, AND EXPECTATIONS

When you consider knowledge, motives, and expectations together, it becomes clearer how relationships begin, develop, grow, and maybe even deteriorate. You initiate a relationship because of your goals and motives (loneliness, stimulation, etc.), and then you form expectations about the person and the relationship based on your level of relational knowledge. This knowledge changes as you interact with your partner and your interactions modify your expectations, which in turn affect your motives for being in the relationship. Relationships are highly dynamic, requiring a continuous assessment of these three elements.

COSTS AND REWARDS OF RELATIONSHIPS

Every relationship produces advantages and disadvantages for the relational partners. Communication researchers Altman and Taylor suggest that relationships begin, develop, grow, and deteriorate based on the rewards and costs that come from the interaction of the two relational partners.[13]

Rewards are those relational elements that you feel good about, whereas **costs** are those that annoy you. When people believe the rewards outweigh the costs, they will most likely find the relationship beneficial and will work to make sure it continues. A person who thinks that the costs are greater than the rewards will most likely not attempt to develop that particular relationship.

Three categories of rewards are available to relational partners:

- **Extrinsic rewards** are gained purely from association with another person. These types of rewards range from new opportunities to "contacts" that may later be useful, to a perceived higher social status. A struggling actor trying to become a star may become involved with a director in show business who can help his career.

- **Instrumental rewards** are those that relational partners give to one another—for example, a basic exchange of goods for services. Two people may decide to live together because one can provide appliances and furniture and the other can provide a steady income to pay the rent.

- **Intrinsic rewards** result from an exchange of intimacy.[14] People looking for these types of rewards are interested in each other for personal reasons. For example, two people who are working out at the local gym may be physically attracted to each other. They may meet later for drinks and eventually develop an intimate relationship.

4 Understanding and Managing Interpersonal Conflicts

When two people communicate while holding different positions on an issue, conflict occurs. **Conflict** is defined by communication researchers Hocker and Wilmot as "an expressed struggle between at least two interdependent parties who perceive incompatible goals, scarce rewards, and interference from the other party in achieving their goals."[1]

At many times in your life, you and another person or persons will have conflicting goals, or you will face competition for scarce resources. You will even encounter people who will attempt to thwart your efforts to achieve important goals. Effective interpersonal communicators manage, rather than minimize or eliminate, conflict in their relationships with others. You may think of managing conflict as bargaining, negotiating, debating, or arguing.

CONDITIONS PRODUCING INTERPERSONAL CONFLICT

Why does conflict occur in relationships? The reasons underlying conflict include:

- incompatible goals,
- unrealistic expectations,
- differing rates of relational growth, and
- inaccurate perceptions and attributions.

Let's explore each of these reasons for conflict in detail.

INCOMPATIBLE GOALS

When two people who must coordinate activities have different ideas about an outcome or end result—incompatible goals—conflict is likely to arise.

Here's a cultural conflict example. Blas Gomez and John Anders are social coordinators for their children's eighth-grade Bar-B-Que Bash. Blas, a native of Bogotá, Colombia, has one set of values about the function, and John, a native Californian, has another. Blas was raised to believe that thirteen-year-old students should be separated by gender, and John's North American culture encourages boys and girls of that age group to "mix and mingle." Because of these two very different outlooks, Blas and John will likely conflict on many issues as they work together. These issues might include how to handle the segregation of genders and which group of children should enter the food line first. Whether Blas and John can manage their incompatible goals will depend on the communication strategies they use.

UNREALISTIC EXPECTATIONS

Conflict can also arise when one or both parties in a relationship have unrealistic expectations. For example, a head football coach, in his first year, expects to reach the playoffs. His main assistant coach, who has been on the staff more than ten years, considers the goal optimistic but unrealistic.

The assistant coach argues that the football team is young and inexperienced, that the players will need some time to adjust to a new strategic philosophy, and that the team faces a difficult schedule. Numerous conflicts occur all year between the two coaches because of their different expectations. While the assistant coach pushes fundamentals and the mastery of basic skills, the head coach pushes the execution of trick plays to ensure victory.

DIFFERING RATES OF RELATIONAL GROWTH

Conflict also occurs when two partners view their relationship as being at different levels or rates of development. For example, Ricky and Shawna have been dating for just under two years. Ricky views the relationship as very serious, having developed strong feelings of love and bonding, anticipating that this is the beginning of a long and happy future together. Shawna views the relationship as primarily "fun." She thinks the couple is just dating, without a long-term commitment or strong expectations for the future.

There can be little question that these partners have progressed in the relationship very differently. You can imagine the many conflicts that will surface between them. There are likely to be disagreements about sex, gifts, attendance at family outings, labels for each other, and even what to say to others about the nature of the relationship.

INACCURATE PERCEPTIONS AND ATTRIBUTIONS

How and what you perceive frequently dictate your impressions, behaviors, and activities. If you are wrong, you are likely to invoke conflict. Consider this incident in which a supervisor, Terry, misperceived two of his newer employees, Bill and Veronica. Terry had heard reports from various people in the company who knew Bill. These reports suggested that Bill was a very bright guy. Veronica had worked in several different departments in the company before reporting to Terry and, unlike Bill, had the reputation of being slow. In actuality, these labels were not only inaccurate but also reversed. Veronica was the bright one, and Bill was slow.

Can you imagine the conflicts that occurred when Terry asked Veronica a question? Rather than deliver a rapid-fire response to Terry, she paused and considered the options or implications. Terry erroneously interpreted this delay as indicative of Veronica's lack of intelligence. Incorrect perceptions about someone else's ability, personality, or behavior can produce serious conflicts because people generally are quick to defend themselves in the face of inaccuracies.

CULTURAL DIFFERENCES IN HANDLING CONFLICT

Different cultures often define and deal with conflict in different ways. Communication researcher Ting-Toomey suggests that high- and low-context cultures manage conflict quite differently.[2] **High-context cultures** are those in which communication is indirect, relies heavily on nonverbal systems, and gives a great deal of meaning to the relationships between communicators. The Japanese, African American, and Latin American cultures are examples of high-context cultures. **Low-context cultures** use more explicit language, are more direct in their meanings, and stress goals and outcomes more than relationships. Examples include the German, Swedish, and English cultures.

Conflict managers in high-context cultures are likely to emphasize harmonious relations rather than personal goals. They will also attempt to maintain "face" for both themselves and the other people in the conflict. Their communication style is more likely to be nonconfrontational, indirect, and concealing. Communicators in low-context cultures manage conflict more directly. They are more confrontational and more goal-oriented rather than being relationally focused, and they are less concerned about "saving face." As you can probably imagine, low-context conflict is more open, volatile, and threatening than high-context conflict. Are you aware of people who live in a low-context culture but who manage conflict as if they lived in a high-context culture?

CONFLICT AS INEVITABLE AND HEALTHY COMMUNICATION

Regardless of how conflicts arise, relationships are stronger when conflicts are managed openly and productively. To begin the discussion of productive conflict, consider some of the assumptions people make about interpersonal conflict. List some of the words and phrases you usually associate with conflict. Does your list contain any of the following behaviors?

- Heated emotions
- Hot temper

- Intolerance
- Shouting and uncontrolled arguing
- Sick stomach
- Red faces
- Clenched fists
- Frustration
- "In-your-face" behavior

If so, you are certainly not alone. These are the behaviors that most people commonly associate with conflict. Think of people who get defensive quickly or who "cannot take a joke" or who take everything "too seriously." Those who act in these ways are prime candidates for unproductive conflict.

The point to stress here is that, although these behaviors may be associated with conflict in some relationships, they do not have to be present in all of them. You can manage conflict by engaging in it productively. **Productive conflict** is based on issues rather than on the participants' personalities. It can and should be conducted without any of the behaviors just mentioned. In fact, when such behaviors are present, the real purpose of conflict is weakened considerably. This occurs because the focus of the conflict turns to individual variables and away from actual issues. A focus on issues is the key to competent conflict management.

If, like many people, you have a negative attitude toward conflict, try to keep an open mind about it. Are you willing to believe that conflict can be productive rather than destructive? To do so, you need to consider the positive outcomes that can result when people disagree and argue. There are several advantages to conflict: decision making, enjoyment of conflict, relational growth, and saving time.

DECISION MAKING

The primary positive outcome of productive conflict is a better decision. When two people get together and fully debate an issue, the chance is far greater that a quality decision will be made. Why? Because conflict provides an arena in which ideas can be tested. Proposed solutions that are logical, workable, economical, and reasonable will stand up during the course of an argument; weaker solutions are likely to be exposed during debate as flawed.

Consider this example: Jack and Bonita have been renting a duplex for the last five years of their seven-year marriage. Jack believes it is now time for the couple to purchase a small home and begin to reap the rewards of that housing investment. If Bonita wants to avoid conflict, she will respond simply "Sure" or "Let's do it." However, this may result in the couple's making a bad decision. In a discussion with Jack, Bonita points out that they have only a limited amount of money in reserve, which the required down payment would significantly diminish; that interest rates are higher now than they are projected to be in the future; that at this time they cannot afford a large enough house; and that the current housing market is to a seller's, not a buyer's, advantage.

Through debate, argument, and conflict, Jack and Bonita finally decide that they will wait two years to purchase a home and that they will put $300 per month in a special savings account earmarked for that purpose. Only through conflict did the flaws in Jack's original proposal emerge. He certainly is glad Bonita spoke up.

Conflict is the essence of decision-making meetings. This is true whether the meeting involves boss–employee, husband–wife, doctor–patient, or any other type of relationship. In fact, if two people who meet to make an important decision are unwilling to engage in conflict or at least consider opposing views, they should not be meeting in the first place. One person should simply have made the decision individually. In strong relationships, the participants introduce and use conflict as a means of reaching satisfying decisions.

ENJOYMENT OF CONFLICT

In order for conflict to be productive rather than destructive, you have to actively engage in it. There is no greater intellectual exercise than exploring and testing ideas with another person. If you are interested in politics, discuss your party's philosophies with one of your friends who is a staunch supporter of the opposition. Through this exchange of conflict, you can have fun and learn a great deal. The key to success in doing this is to avoid taking your partner's arguments personally.

You might even think of conflict as a sport in which ideas, rather than a ball, are tossed between the participants. A healthy attitude toward conflict is marked by a special kind of enjoyment that is created when two participants share ideas.

RELATIONAL GROWTH

Conflict helps a relationship develop. As two people begin to explore issues together, trust and respect are fostered. For example, Isaac didn't like the way Mary shopped for groceries. He always thought she spent too much. Mary had always believed that quality products simply cost more. When Isaac confronted Mary on the issue and they discussed it, Mary's respect and attraction for Isaac increased dramatically. Mary's desires to please herself and her partner were virtually equal, and Isaac's concern helped build a communication style they had not previously explored. They were pleased to discover that there were ways that both of them could be satisfied. The relationship seemed to come alive in ways that would never have occurred without conflict. As a result, the couple began to talk about and work through more issues than ever before. Rather than having a relationship in which either partner suppressed feelings, anger, or resentment, the couple became much more open, which led to a stronger, healthier union.

SAVING TIME

You may think that you save time when you reach a decision without questioning, arguing, or debating. That is certainly true. Meetings in which conflict is suppressed or avoided are shorter than those in which conflict is encouraged and allowed to run its course. Unfortunately, many decisions made in the absence of conflict are poor and require much more time later to correct. Had the time been taken at the outset to make a proper decision through productive conflict, less time would have been spent in the long term.

For example, several years ago, in a major company, a decision was reached to radically alter the way presentations were made to major customers and suppliers. For years, the accepted style was to present information on slides, using two screens, projecting one image to the left of the speaker and a separate image on the screen to the right. One day, a top executive made a unilateral decision that henceforth all presentations would be given using only one screen and one projected image at a time.

After the order was implemented, problems cropped up immediately. Speakers who had used the old style for years had great difficulty adapting to the new technique. Standard presentations that were established for the two-screen method had to be reorganized to fit the new format. Even the seating arrangements for large meetings had to be altered so that everyone could see a single screen. After the new method had been in use for about eighteen months, a task force was created to review the decision. When the committee recommended a return to the old format, everyone accepted the idea. Permanent presentations that had been created in this interim period had to be reorganized. Managers who had joined the company in the last year and a half had to undergo special training to learn the old two-screen format. Obviously, much time and effort could have been saved had the task force met at the outset to study the issue. Through productive conflict, debate, and argument, the group could have uncovered the flaws in the proposed one-screen design.

A MODEL OF EFFECTIVE CONFLICT MANAGEMENT

Effective, productive conflict can be divided into six distinct phases:

- prelude
- assessment
- engagement

- action
- decision
- reflection

Following these phases will help you to operate rationally rather than emotionally. Moreover, you will be more likely to approach the topic proactively rather than reactively. Finally, and most important, you will focus the conflict on the issue and not on the other person.

PRELUDE

Conflict does not simply "happen." As you have seen, conflict has many sources. In addition, you and your conflict partners bring your own personality traits, tendencies, predispositions, and conflict styles to conflict episodes. You also cannot forget that conflict takes place within a relational context. The status of a relationship is a very important factor that affects many conflict behaviors. In short, the first phase of conflict actually begins before any words are spoken. The prelude phase of this model is influenced by three factors:

- traits
- relational status
- style

Let's explore each in depth.

Traits

Traits — individual characteristics that typically do not vary from situation to situation; they are either physical (e.g., height, weight, eyesight) or psychological (e.g., open-mindedness, friendliness, intelligence) — play a key role in conflict situations.

Argumentativeness is one such trait. According to the findings of communication researcher Infante, people who are highly argumentative typically do the following three things:[3]

- Recognize issues that are "ripe" for controversy
- Take positions on those issues and provide evidence and reasoning to support their positions
- Refute others' positions if these are counter to their own

The more an individual uses these three behaviors, the more argumentative the person is. Conversely, the less someone engages in these behaviors, the less argumentative he or she is.

Individuals who enjoy arguing or debating with others on issues are also likely to be favorably disposed to productive conflict. People who are argumentative focus their arguments on the issue or argument at hand instead of the individuals arguing. Argumentativeness is thus a positive trait for individuals to exhibit in conflict situations.

In contrast, **verbal aggressiveness**—another type of trait—is a negative influence in conflict situations. People who are verbally aggressive focus their arguments on individuals in addition to, or instead of, issues.

When you are in a conflict situation with a person who is verbally aggressive, you typically encounter undesirable behaviors, especially name-calling, "mudslinging," or the reintroduction of downgrading examples from the relationship's past. One study by Infante and Wigely found that people who are deficient in argumentative skills often resort to verbal aggressiveness, because personal attacks may be the only way they can deal with another person in a conflict situation.[4]

To help you see the difference between argumentativeness and verbal aggressiveness, suppose that two supervisors are discussing whether only English should be spoken in the workplace. They have opposing views: Ms. Sanders believes that if people want to live and work in North America, they should speak English, whereas Ms. King believes that the mixture of ethnicities is what makes North America unique. Which supervisor is verbally aggressive? Argumentative?

MS. SANDERS: If foreigners want to live in the United States, they should speak my language. I want to know if they're talking and laughing about me when I pass by them. It's like these people have their own code.

MS. KING: As far as I'm concerned, if they perform their work on time and we're able to communicate in a work situation, they can speak, sing, or whistle in their native tongues while performing their tasks.

MS. SANDERS: Well, you must be an anti-American foreigner-lover.

MS. KING: I believe that since we all originated from various continents, we're all foreigners, except for the Native Americans.

People in conflict should take the high road and use argumentativeness instead of aggressiveness. With argumentativeness, an issue can be left at the conflict table, and two people can then carry on their relationship in a normal manner. A relationship may be harmed, however, if verbal aggressiveness is used.

Another trait that affects conflict is the degree to which one or more of the partners possesses **communication apprehension**. Communication researcher McCroskey has defined communication apprehension (CA) as fear or anxiety about real or anticipated communication with another person or persons.[5] A partner may possess good arguments, rational data, exceptional reasoning, and strong stances, but may simply be too apprehensive to deliver them.

Relational Status

A major factor that can produce profound differences in conflict is the status of a relationship. It is important to consider the relationship factor because relationships change as a result of how conflict is handled. As you refine your relational schemas about another person, you gain a greater understanding of three factors involving conflict and relationships:

- **Valence.** Valence refers to the feelings of satisfaction with the communication that takes place in a relationship. When the partners in a relationship are satisfied and pleased with their interaction, the communication has a positive valence. Conversely, if the interaction produces dissatisfaction and displeasure, communication has a negative valence. Three different pairs of valences are possible in a relationship, and conflict is affected differently by each. One possibility is that *both participants are dissatisfied* with the communication that takes place in the relationship. In this kind of context, conflict is likely to fare very poorly. Because the partners do not even enjoy talking with each other under nonargumentative or nonconfrontive circumstances, the topics on which they have conflict are not likely to produce enjoyment either. When *one participant is happy with the communication in the relationship and the other is not*, any conflict that occurs is either going to help strengthen the bonds between the two, or weaken the ties between them. When *both partners are pleased with the communication* between them, valence is at its highest and productive conflict has an excellent chance of succeeding.

- **Stability.** Stability is measured by the degree to which a relationship experiences "peaks and valleys." All relationships have good times and bad times. The more consistent a relationship is, the more stability it has. Stable relationships provide the best context for productive argument.

- **Power.** The distribution of power in a relationship also affects conflict. When one partner has power over another, the kind of conflict is likely to be very different from the conflict between equals. Conversely, when the partners have equal status, there is very little that one partner can "hold" over the other. As a result, both partners are likely to initiate conflict at about the same rate. The refutation, argument, debate, and questioning that take place will probably be much more open and profound. Consent will occur because one partner is convinced of an argument, not because the other has power. Power is not limited to simple hierarchical differences. In many relationships, people have power because you give it to them. Therefore, any person who controls resources that you desire has power over you. This is true whether the partner controls money you want, equipment you want to borrow, or even sex. Conflict with a person who holds power over you for any reason will likely be very different from conflict situations in which power is equal.

Style

Every individual who engages in conflict prefers certain behaviors over others. These preferences define your style.

Five conflict styles are assessed by the Thomas-Kilmann Conflict Management of Differences (MODE) survey.[6] These styles vary according to the degree to which an individual is assertive or cooperative. **Assertiveness** is defined as emphasizing your own concerns and taking action to achieve your goals; **cooperativeness** is defined as emphasizing the other's concerns and working toward shared goals. The five styles are:

- Collaborating—highly assertive and cooperative
- Compromising—moderately assertive and cooperative
- Competing—assertive and uncooperative
- Accommodating—unassertive and cooperative
- Avoiding—unassertive and uncooperative

Although you might vary your conflict style for some people and some topics, for the most part people's styles are fairly consistent. The biggest factor that produces a change in style is probably the degree to which a topic or person is important to you. You may find, for example, that you behave differently in conflicts that arise about where you should live once you graduate versus what kind of movie you should attend. You may also find that you behave differently in conflicts with your best friend than you do with your boss. Nonetheless, most people have the same predispositions or tendencies toward conflict regardless of the topic or person involved.

ASSESSMENT

Before engaging in communication during a conflict situation, competent participants conduct a thorough assessment of their own needs and those that they believe are important to their partner. In public speaking, speakers must analyze the audience and make certain adjustments based on whom they are addressing. Failure to do so may prove disastrous for the speakers. This same assessment should be performed prior to a conflict situation with a partner. Let us now look at some of the items that should be assessed in this phase, including:

- personal goals
- the other's goals
- relational goals
- "win-win" as the ultimate goal

Personal Goals

Your own goals and objectives are very important in any conflict situation; without them, you would not have any stake in the discussion. There are several questions that you should consider in advance. For example: When you enter into the conflict, what are you likely to gain? To lose? What do you desire as an outcome? How important is that outcome to you? What positions do you plan to advance during the discussion? Can you substantiate your positions?

The Other's Goals

You are not the only one who has goals and objectives in a conflict situation; your partner has them too. Unless you consider what these goals and objectives are, you are likely to be unsuccessful in influencing your partner. What is your partner's probable reaction to the conflict? How do your partner's interests differ from your own? What issue do you think is most important to your partner? What kind of experiences or background does the partner bring to this situation?

Relational Goals

Conflict does not take place in a vacuum. Whatever happens through conflict affects a relationship. As you know, a relationship may grow stronger if the conflict is productive. If the conflict is personal instead of issue based, the relationship may be adversely affected.

Before beginning a conversation that involves conflict, participants should consider the effect the argument or debate is likely to have on their relationship. Has this issue been discussed before? If so, what has been discussed and how? Is there any new information? If not, how much do you need to educate your partner prior to the discussion?

Is the topic one in which your partner's ego is heavily involved? Is your partner more knowledgeable about the issue than you are? What adjustments might you need to make in order to convince your partner that your position is the better one for the relationship?

"Win-Win" as the Ultimate Goal

The best reason to engage in conflict is to allow both participants to gain from the discussion. When this occurs, the conflict has been successful. This is called "**win-win**" and refers to the idea that both parties can meet their own goals and those for their relationship from the conflict situation.

The win-win philosophy of conflict means that you not only look out for yourself during an argument but that you also monitor the role and status of the other party. This ensures that both of you receive substantive outcomes from your efforts in the conversation. This is parallel to the collaboration style of conflict mentioned in the last section.

ENGAGEMENT

In the third phase of conflict, engagement, the partners create a context for conflict. The physical location of a conflict as well as each participant's psychological readiness are very important. In many cases, one partner must actually entice the other into engaging in conflict. During engagement, two important factors are dealt with:

- decreasing resistance, and
- clarifying and focusing on issues.

Decreasing Resistance
One of the greatest barriers to productive conflict occurs when one of the partners does not want to participate in a debate. Here are some reasons why people may be reluctant to engage in conflict:

- They do not see any alternatives to a solution that seems obvious to them.
- They do not consider the issue complex enough to merit argument.
- They do not enjoy arguing or debating issues.
- They are concerned that the relationship is not strong enough to endure argument.
- They do not believe that the time or place is right for conflict.

Clarifying and Focusing on Issues
We have already noted that effective interepersonal communicators engage in productive conflict—conflict that is based on issues and not on the personalities of the participants. One of the most important steps a communicator takes at the outset of conflict is to steer the conversation toward substantive issues. If this step does not take place, the conflict may get off to a very bad start and may never recover.

One of the best ways to safeguard the civilized tone of any encounter is to begin with statements that erase or minimize any link between the issue under discussion and the individual who is delivering a position on it. Here are some examples you might use:

- "I don't want you to take this personally. We need to talk about . . ."
- "I know that you have put a lot of time and energy into this project and that it's very important to you. But I think you should step back a little and look at this a different way."
- "You have some strong views on this matter. I respect those views, and I want to listen to what you have to say. But there are some other pieces to the puzzle that I don't think you have considered."

Statements such as these can also be used during the course of the conversation in which the conflict takes place. They can be very important in refocusing the conflict on the issue being discussed. On some occasions you may need to be even more direct:

- "I'm sorry you are offended by what I said. I wasn't talking about you. I was talking about the position you've taken."
- "No, I would have said the same thing no matter who brought it up."

Competent communicators in conflict situations not only keep themselves focused on issues but also help to keep their partners focused on the subjects being discussed.

ACTION

The action phase includes the "how" and "what" of conflict. The how involves the selection of strategies that a communicator uses in a conflict situation. The what involves the tactics, or messages, that are used to enact the strategies. In addition, competent communicators are aware of several traps that can move a conflict in unproductive directions.

The How: Strategies for Engaging in Productive Conflict

One of the first determinations you need to make is to decide what is most important to you: your own goals, your partner's goals, or your relationship's goals. This decision is very important because you cannot have it all three ways.

First, let's look at three types of *strategies*:

- **Cooperative strategies.** These are strategies in which the communicative partners work together to maximize the goals of each person and objectives of the relationship. The important factor is not whether you win or lose but rather what is the best outcome for both partners in the relationship.

- **Obstinate or unyielding strategies.** Obstinate or unyielding strategies promote the objectives of an individual, as opposed to those of a relational partner. In these strategies, partners are self-centered and individualistic in their approach to attaining goals, and the impact on the relationship is not considered very important.

- **Escapist strategies.** Escapist strategies attempt to prevent direct conflict. In some cases, this is simply avoidance. In other cases, participants attempt to postpone conflict, change topics, or pass responsibility to other people. The objective of this strategy is simply to ensure that conflict does not take place.

You will notice that these three general strategies take very different directions and are associated with different kinds of communication behaviors. Look at a simple but common example.

Suppose that Lisa and Kathy ordered only one piece of lemon meringue pie at a restaurant to eat after their dinner. If you were to go inside their minds, both Lisa and Kathy would like to eat the pie. In discussing who gets the pie, if Lisa used a cooperative strategy, she would probably ask Kathy, "Would you like to split the pie?" This tactic would consider the feelings of both participants. Conversely, if Lisa used an obstinate strategy, she might argue, "I am not on a diet, so I deserve the pie." If she used an escapist strategy, Lisa might simply say, "Kathy, go ahead and eat the lemon pie," even though she really wanted it.

The What: Tactics for Engaging in Productive Conflict

Now, let's look at specific message-based *tactics* that will help you put your strategies in motion:

- **Probing.** Probe for clarifications and explanations from your partner. Don't be satisfied with general positions or vague and ambiguous answers. Ask probing questions that force the individual to be more specific and pointed. Try to find out your partner's motivations, goals, and attitudes toward you and the conflict issue. ("What do you mean?" "Can you give me an example?" "What's at risk for me? For you?") If you suspect that your partner is not being truthful, probing may be an appropriate tactic, as it can cause your partner to be less deceitful. In many cases, the more you probe, the less your partner has to say and the more obvious these behaviors become.

- **Debating/Arguing.** Productive conflict depends on debate and argument. Clearly, debate and argument do not mean yelling and shouting. You can argue and debate either by taking a devil's advocate position, and/or by arguing against analogies. Before agreeing on an issue, play devil's advocate by asking what the worst-case scenario would be. A devil's advocate may bring up questions such as: What is the most money that could be lost? How much time could possibly be wasted? What is the longest distance we would have to travel? If the answer your partner gives to these types of questions is unsatisfying to you, certainly other alternatives must be generated and explored. Second, argue against analogies that the other person offers to support a position. An analogy simply indicates that what is true in one instance will be true in another. When you hear people say, "It's just like . . ." or "It's no different from . . .," they are using analogies. For productive conflict to take place, you need to demonstrate that the differences between the instances or cases that are being compared are so significant that the analogy is invalid.

- **Bargaining.** Bargaining tactics constitute a special form of conflict. In bargaining, the partners argue for their respective positions within mutually agreed upon guidelines. You are probably most familiar with the bargaining tactics used in union and labor negotiations or courtroom bargaining pleas. Each side agrees to certain rules and procedures when arguing its case. Many conflict situations that you will face may resemble bargaining sessions, and it is a good idea to become competent in bargaining tactics. Bargaining tactics are very much like the conflict strategies discussed earlier (cooperative, obstinate, and escapist strategies).

- **Making threats and promises.** Threats are expressed intentions to behave in ways that are detrimental to the other party if that person does not comply with certain requests or terms. Conversely, promises are expressed intentions to behave in ways that are beneficial to the other party in return for compliance with certain requests or terms. Threats and promises can sometimes provoke conflicts. When threatened, many people retaliate rather than consent. A promise, especially from someone who has a bad history of keeping promises, can cause all kinds of problems. However, threats and promises can also resolve conflicts. In the heat of an argument between two people, a well-placed threat or promise may put an end to a discussion.

- **Face saving.** If one or more people get together in an atmosphere where the "best solution" wins, the victor is not the person but the solution. In this atmosphere, no one needs to save face. Additionally, the parties should try to minimize any defensiveness or retaliation that is associated with winning or losing an argument. These responses come about because someone is concerned about having an undesirable image or making an undesirable impression. Finally, to save face, a party must be able to have a "way out" of a position. There is no reason to devastate the other person even if you win the conflict. Instead, you can offer to support your partner in other situations.

- **Summarizing.** Summarizing gives your partner the chance to disagree, clarify a point, or amplify any part of the discussion before it moves on to another subtopic. Statements such as "Here's what I think we've said so far" or "What we have agreed to is" are extremely useful in keeping a discussion on track. The major advantage here is that the topic is still fresh in the participants' minds. If one partner has a different opinion, perception, or recollection of what was discussed, the best time to make a correction is right then, not ten minutes, one hour, one week, or six months later.

- **Compromising.** Compromise tactics are used often in relationships because they are quick and simple methods of reaching a conclusion or a result. The focus of compromise is on reaching a quick decision by agreeing on the method of deciding. Settling for a compromise rather than working through issues is not the most productive way to manage conflict in a relationship. But compromise is helpful in certain circumstances, such as when a decision must be made under severe time constraints. In that situation, there is no time to engage in active debate, argument, or questioning. You should also resort to compromise when the outcomes are relatively unimportant to you and your partner. Why not just split the difference when conflict is not worth the effort?

DECISION

The fifth phase of conflict involves agreeing on a **consensus** decision. In this phase, the exact agreement must be clearly summarized and reiterated to avoid all disagreement about what the final conclusion is. In some cases, the participants actually sign a contract or other formal document.

CHECKLIST

Effective Bargaining Strategies

The key to bargaining is to develop a strategy that supports a favorable position for your side while promoting the value of your adversary's point of view. Based on research findings, the following steps can lead to a successful bargaining strategy.

✓ Begin with high but realistic offers. Starting high allows you to "give" some later.

✓ Present beginning offers in a cooperative manner so that adversaries know you can be reasonable.

✓ Clear obstacles by compromising a little on your initial offer.

✓ Stand your ground when you feel the opposition is taking advantage of your good faith.

✓ Remain committed and enthusiastic about your goals throughout the bargaining session.

✓ Know what you are talking about. Be well informed about your own position and your adversary's position. Don't get caught off guard by something you ought to know about.

✓ Let the opposition know that you understand its position and are sensitive to its needs.

✓ Avoid obstinate and escapist tactics unless these are absolutely necessary. Seldom do these behaviors serve a useful purpose.[7]

Reaching a Consensus

Once all the positions have been advanced, data have been given, and reasoning has been proposed, the participants must reach a conclusion. Reaching this decision is what the conversation that involved conflict is all about. Consensus, defined as a mutually satisfying agreement reached by two or more parties, is very different from compromise (whose focus is on a quick decision).

Before the parties to a conflict "sign on the dotted line," the following three factors should be considered:

- **Goals.** Do both parties meet their goals and objectives through this decision? If not, the decision will not be the win-win outcome discussed previously.

- **Partner.** Does each partner recognize the benefits gained from the conflict? If there are any concerns, these should be pointed out before the discussion is brought to a close.

- **Relationship.** How is the relationship different as a result of the conflict? Is it stronger? Weaker? Are there topics that were alluded to but not discussed—topics that should be considered in a future conversation?

Summary and Confirmation

In some conflict situations, the parties must actually reach a formal agreement such as signing a contract or other legal document. In other situations, the outcome is far less formal. Regardless of the situation, summarizing and confirming the outcome is an extremely important step. In all conversations involving conflict, at least one of the participants should summarize the conversation. When someone says, "So, our agreement is . . ." or "What we have decided to do is . . . ," then there is no room for confusion.

In some cases, one or both parties must engage in a series of follow-up steps. Even these behaviors must be agreed upon at the conclusion of a conflict-based conversation, or they may never be performed. One person may say, "So you have agreed to do these things by . . ." or "We have six steps still to take. Let me read them to be sure we agree."

REFLECTION

Resolution of the conflict does not mean it is over. Reflection, the sixth and final phase of productive conflict, is extremely important. It requires the participants to evaluate their behavior during the conflict situation and to assess the impact of the conflict on their relationship. The participants must consider their strengths and weaknesses in the various skills they used during the conflict situation. Furthermore, they must decide what impact the conflict has had on their feelings about the other person. In some cases the relationship is stronger, and in other cases some repair work needs to be done. The final phase of this model, then, is concerned with what happens afterward. You should look at two important factors: the relationship and the performance of communication.

Reevaluating the Relationship

Because conflict between two people takes place in a relational context, you can be assured that the relationship is different afterward. In many cases, the relationship is stronger, especially when the conflict has centered on the issues. The partners should capitalize on this advantage and find other topics or areas of concern that can be worked through together.

Assessing Your Communication Effectiveness and Performance

Another factor to consider after the conflict has concluded is the degree to which you performed effectively as a communicator. Assess your behavior and try to discover some skills that you need to improve. For example, how well did you really listen to your partner? Did you ask your partner clear and concise questions? How strong were your arguments? Did your data support the positions you took? Were you able to substantiate each of your claims? Were you able to focus on issues instead of your partner's personality or past behavior? Did you lose your temper at any time?

Exactly what is competence in conflict situations? Competence in communicating was defined earlier as effectively attaining goals in a manner appropriate to the context of the relationship. The context of a relationship can be defined in many ways, including maturity of the participants, length of the relationship, status differences or similarities, and type of relationship (such as business or romantic).

Demonstrating mastery in interpersonal conflict can be quite difficult. Conflict often exists because of the presence of incompatible goals. The participants must seek a successful outcome while considering each other's expectations for the relationship and the situation. Considering that most of these situations are emotion-laden, there is always the potential for inappropriate behavior.[8]

One tool that separates competent from incompetent participants in conflict is the versatility that each person brings to the situation. Versatile individuals, with a repertoire of all types of communication behaviors, can respond with greater flexibility than can those who typically behave in only one way.

The key to competence, however, is more than just possessing the ability to communicate in different ways. Competence requires the individual to communicate in the appropriate way, given situational demands. A person may be able to be sarcastic as well as serious, but how and under what circumstances these behaviors are used is the key to his or her competence. A flexible person who uses the wrong behaviors in certain circumstances is just as incompetent as an inflexible person who cannot use the behavior at all.

CHECKLIST:

Steps Toward Effective Interpersonal Communication

✓ Identify the goals people have as they develop relationships.

✓ Explain the information-seeking strategies people use to reduce uncertainty in relationships.

✓ Identify the phases of interpersonal relationships.

✓ Describe the factors that lead to relational decline.

✓ Assess the rewards and costs of relationships.

✓ Distinguish between productive and destructive conflict.

# GLOSSARY

adapter   A movement or gesture that satisfies some physical or psychological need.

affect display   An unintentional movement or expression that conveys a mood or emotional state.

affiliation   Feelings for another, ranging from love (high positive affiliation) to hate (high negative affiliation); one of the three primary functions of communication.

appropriate communication   In an interpersonal communication context, behavior that meets the expectations of one's specific communication partner, other people in one's immediate presence, and the demands of the situation. Expectations of appropriate behavior are formed in large part by cultural norms and rules.

argumentativeness   A conflict style that seeks out controversial issues and revels in debating them.

artifacts   An accessory used for decoration or identification.

assertiveness   A conflict style that emphasizes personal concerns.

association   Association can be seen as a relationship with an acquaintance rather than as a true friendship. An associative friendship is most likely to develop between people who have frequent contact, such as co-workers, classmates, or neighbors.

audience   One or more people who are listening to what a person is saying and/or watching what that person is doing.

chronemics   The communicative ability of the use of time.

code   The symbols, signals, or signs used to construct messages.

communication   A process defined by six characteristics: (1) symbolic behavior, (2) the sharing of a code, (3) its tie to culture, (4) intentionality, (5) the presence of a medium, and (6) the fact that it is transactional.

communication apprehension   Fear or anxiety associated with real or anticipated communication with another person or persons.

communication relationship   An interdependence of two or more people that is based on symbolic exchange.

conflict   A struggle between two or more interdependent parties who perceive incompatible goals, scarce rewards, and interference from the other party or parties in achieving their goals.

consensus   A mutually satisfying agreement reached by two or more parties.

control   The ability of one person to influence another person or persons and the manner in which their relationship is conducted; one of the three primary functions of communication.

cooperativeness   A conflict style that emphasizes the other's concerns.

culture   The shared beliefs, values, and practices of a group of people.

decline   The fifth of six possible stages in relational development, decline is the erosion that occurs over time to some relationships.

decode   Physically receive a message (or other type of stimulus) and interpret and assign meaning to it.

effective communication   Communication that helps you to meet your goals.

emblem   A movement or gesture that has a direct verbal translation and is displayed to replace words.

emotional stimulation   In interpersonal communication, a form of stimulation involving the expression of emotions, the opportunity for which is provided by the bond between two people in a relationship. (See also **intellectual stimulation** and **physical stimulation.**)

encode   Mentally construct and physically produce a message.

expectations   An intuitive thought or conscious desire in regard to an upcoming encounter.

exploration   The second of six possible stages of relational development; the information-seeking stage.

family   A social group whose members are related by blood, marriage, or adoption; have specified roles (e.g., husband, wife, son, mother) and statuses; and usually share a common residence and cooperate economically.

friendship   A relationship between two or more people that is perceived as mutually satisfying, productive, and beneficial.

functional perspective   A focus on what kinds of communication behaviors work for people, and why they work, in various situations.

goal achievement   Focusing attention on the task at hand in order to achieve a goal; one of the three primary functions of communication. Also called **task orientation.**

haptics   Touching behavior.

high-context cultures   A culture that avoids the use of direct language, relying more on context to convey meaning.

illustrator   A movement or gesture that accompanies and illustrates a verbal message.

initiation   The first of six possible stages of relational development, in which expectations and knowledge are based on general information gained from the partner's appearance, demeanor, and behavior.

intellectual stimulation   In interpersonal communication, a form of stimulation stemming from conversations about topics of shared interest, especially current events, movies, books, and societal issues. (See also **emotional stimulation** and **physical stimulation.**)

intensification   The third of six possible stages of relational development, in which the partners are more likely to focus on the relationship, instead of simply seeking personal information about each other. This is the stage in which relational intimacy may be felt for the first time.

intentionality   A term that refers to a level of consciousness or purposefulness of a communicator in the encoding of messages.

interpersonal communication   The process of two or three people exchanging messages in order to share meaning, create understanding, and develop relationships.

interpretation   In a communication context, the third step we use to organize our perceptions in a meaningful way. In this step, we interpret meaningful patterns, using our past experiences, assumptions, knowledge, and feelings. (See also **selection** and **organization.**)

intimacy   A deep understanding of another person; one of the highest levels that a relationship can aspire to.

kinesics   The communicative ability of gestures and body movements.

language   A symbol system used to think about and communicate experiences and feelings.

listening   The process of recognizing, understanding, and accurately interpreting the messages communicated by others.

love   A deep affection for and attraction to another person; generally involves a relationship that is more exclusive than friendship.

low-context cultures   A culture that relies more on the use of direct language than on the nuances of context to impart meaning.

medium   A vehicle to transport or carry the symbols in communication.

mutual satisfaction   A win-win situation in which a communication interaction optimizes outcomes for both partners.

nonverbal communication   The process of signaling meaning through behavior that does not involve the content of spoken words.

oculesics   Communicative eye behavior.

olfatics   The communicative characteristics of smells.

organization   In a communication context, the second step we use to organize our perceptions in a meaningful way. In this step, we organize the stimuli we have selected into meaningful patterns. (See also **selection** and **interpretation**.)

outcome   The product or end state of a communication encounter or series of encounters.

outcome-oriented   A definition of interpersonal communication that holds that we communicate with some purpose in mind—whether conscious or subconscious.

paralanguage   The communicative value of vocal behavior; the meaning of how something is said.

perception   The way in which you make sense of the world around you.

physical stimulation   In interpersonal communication, fulfillment of the human need to touch and be touched. (See also **emotional stimulation** and **intellectual stimulation**.)

prelude   The first of six phases in productive conflict.

process   The manner in which a communication encounter is conducted.

productive conflict   Disagreement that results in a positive outcome because it is based on issues rather than on the participants' personalities.

proxemics   The communicative aspects of the use of space.

receiver   The person, group, or organization that decodes a message or other type of stimulus.

receptivity   A type of friendship in which one partner is the primary giver and the other is the primary taker.

reciprocity   A type of friendship that involves self-surrender, loyalty, mutual respect, affection, and support, and in which the partners give and take equally and share responsibility for maintaining the relationship.

regulator   A movement or gesture that regulates conversation.

relational history   The sum of the "objective" events in a relationship and the shared experiences of relational partners; also, the set of thoughts, perceptions, and impressions one has formed about one's previous relational partners.

relational knowledge   Information you gain through your experiences in relationships.

relational schemas   Information used to interpret messages received in a relationship.

relationship   The interdependence of two or more people in order to achieve some goal.

rewards   In an interpersonal communication context, rewards are those relational elements that you feel good about.

selection   In a communication context, the first step we use to organize our perceptions in a meaningful way. In this step, we select certain stimuli from the environment around us. (See also **organization** and **interpretation**.)

self-concept   The awareness and understanding of who one is as interpreted and influenced by one's thoughts, actions, abilities, values, goals, and ideals, and by other people.

sender   The person, group, or organization that encodes a message or produces a stimulus.

stabilization   The third of six possible stages of relational development; the stage in which the relationship is no longer volatile or temporary. In this stage, the partners have a great deal of knowledge about one another, their expectations are accurate and realistic, and they feel comfortable with their motives for being in the relationship.

symbol   A sign (usually a word) used to describe a person, idea, or thing (a referent).

symbolic behavior   Behavior that uses a shared symbol system.

task orientation   *See* goal achievement.

termination   In an interpersonal communication context, the end of a relationship. The last of six possible stages in relationship development.

time orientation   Time preferences that may be psychologically, biologically, or culturally based.

traits   Individual physical and psychological characteristics that typically do not vary from situation to situation.

transactional process   A process in which two or more people exchange speaker and listener roles, and in which the behavior of each person is dependent on and influenced by the behavior of the other.

verbal aggressiveness   A conflict style that involves attacking the other party's self-concept.

vocalization   A vocal cue that does not have the structure of language.

voice qualities   The vocal cues of tempo; resonance; rhythm, articulation, pitch, and glottis control; and pitch range.

win-win   A situation in which both parties benefit. Specifically used to refer to productive conflict in interpersonal communication.

zero-sum matter   A situation in which the more control one party has, the less control the other party has.

# NOTES

CHAPTER 1

1. F. E. X. Dance and C. Larson, *Functions of Human Communication: A Theoretical Approach* (New York: Holt, Rinehart and Wintson, 1976).
2. P. Ekman and W. B. Friesen, *Unmasking the Face* (Englewood Cliffs, NJ: Prentice-Hall, 1975).
3. B. Whorf, *Language, Thought, and Reality* (New York: John Wiley and Sons, 1956).
4. E. T. Hall, *The Silent Language* (Greenwich, CT: Fawcett Publications, 1959); and E. T. Hall, *The Hidden Dimension* (Garden City, NY: Doubleday, 1966).
5. R. Buck, "Emotional Education and Mass Media: A New View of the Global Village," in *Advancing Communication Science: Merging Mass and Interpersonal Processes*, eds. R. P. Hawkins, J. M. Wiemann, and S. Pingree (Beverly Hills, CA: Sage, 1988), 44–76; G. Cronkhite, "On the Focus, Scope, and Coherence of the Study of Human Symbolic Activity," *Quarterly Journal of Speech* 3 (1986): 231–43; M. T. Motley, "On Whether One Can(Not) Communicate: An Examination via Traditional Communication Postulates," *Western Journal of Speech Communication,* 56 (1990): 1–20.
6. E. Goffman, *Interaction Ritual: Essays on Face-to-Face Behavior* (Garden City, NY: Doubleday, 1967).
7. B. O'Keefe and S.A. McCormack, "Message Design Logic and Message Goal Structure: Effects on Perceptions of Message Quality in Regulative Communication Situations," *Human Communication Research* 14 (1987): 68–85. Also see D. J. Canary, M. J. Cody, and S. Smith, "Compliance-Gaining Goals: An Inductive Analysis of Actors' Goal Types, Strategies, and Successes," in *Strategic Interpersonal Communication*, eds. J. A. Daly and J. M. Wiemann (Hillsdale, NJ: Lawrence Erlbaum, 1994), 33–90.

CHAPTER 2

1. J. C. McCroskey, "The Communication Apprehension Perspective," in *Avoiding Communication: Shyness, Reticence, and Communication Apprehension*, eds. J. A. Daly and J. C. McCroskey (Beverly Hills, CA: Sage, 1984), 13–38.
2. D. Cegala, "Interaction Involvement: A Cognitive Dimension of Communicative Competence," *Communication Education* 30 (1981): 109–21.
3. R. Edwards, "Sensitivity to Feedback and the Development of Self," *Communication Quarterly* 38 (1990): 101–11.
4. D. Morris, *Bodywatching* (New York: Crown, 1985).
5. P. Eckman, W. Friesen, and R. Ellsworth, *Emotion in the Human Face: Guidelines for Research and an Integration of Findings* (New York: Pergamon, 1972).
6. D. Leathers, *Successful Nonverbal Communication: Principles and Applications* (New York: Macmillan, 1986).
7. M. L. Knapp and J. A. Hall, *Nonverbal Communication in Human Interaction* (Fort Worth, TX: Holt, Rinehart and Winston, 1992); D. W. Addington, "The Relationship of Selected Vocal Characteristics to Personality Perception," *Speech Monographs* 35 (1968): 492–503.

8. B. Goss and D. O'Hair, *Communicating in Interpersonal Relationships* (New York: Macmillan Publishing Company, 1988).
9. E. Hall, *The Silent Language* (New York: Doubleday, 1959).
10. J. K. Burgoon, D. B. Buller, and W. G. Woodall, *Nonverbal Communication: The Unspoken Dialogue* (New York: Harper and Row, 1989).
11. V. P. Richmond, J. C. McCroskey, and S. K. Payne, *Nonverbal Behavior in Interpersonal Relations*, 190–91.
12. L. K. Steil, L. L. Barker, and K. W. Watson, *Effective Listening: Key to Success* (Reading, MA: Addison-Wesley, 1983); F. I. Wolff, N. C. Marsnik, W. S. Tacey, and R. G. Nichols, *Perceptive Listening* (New York: Holt, Rinehart & Winston, 1983).

CHAPTER 3

1. S. Panalp, "Relational Schemata: A Test of Alternative Forms of Relational Knowledge as Guides to Communication," *Human Communications Research*, 12 (1985): 3–29.
2. J. C. Pearson and B. H. Spitzberg, *Interpersonal Communication: Concepts, Components, and Contexts*, 2nd ed. (Dubuque, IA: Wm. C. Brown, 1990).
3. J. Reisman, *Anatomy of Friendship* (Lexington, MA: Lexis Publishers, 1979).
4. G. D. Nass and G. W. McDonald, *Marriage and the Family* (New York: Random House, 1982).
5. This model is based on the following research: G. Miller and M. Steinberg, *Between People* (Palo Alto, CA: Science Research Associates, 1975); I. Altman and D. Taylor, *Social Penetration Theory* (New York: Holt, Rinehart and Winston, 1973); M. L. Knapp and A. L. Vangelisti, *Interpersonal Communication and Human Relationships*, 2nd ed. (Boston: Allyn & Bacon, 1992).
6. W. Wilmot, "Relationship Stages: Initiation and Stabilization," in *Contexts of Communication*, ed. J. Civikly (New York: Holt, Rinehart & Winston, 1981).
7. M. L. Knapp and A. Vangelisti, *Interpersonal Communication and Human Relationships* (Boston: Pearson Allyn & Bacon, 1995).
8. E. Goffman, *Relations in Public* (New York: Harper & Row, 1971).
9. Knapp and Vangelisti, *Interpersonal Communication and Human Relationships*.
10. B. Goss and D. O'Hair, *Communicating in Interpersonal Relationships*. (New York: Macmillan, 1988).
11. M. S. Davis, *Intimate Relations* (New York: Free Press, 1973), 245–83.
12. J. H. Harvey, T. L. Orbuch, and A. L. Weber, "A Social Psychological Model of Account-Making in Response to Severe Stress," *Journal of Language and Social Psychology* 9 (1990): 191–207; J. H. Harvey, G. Agostinelli, and A. L. Weber, "Account-Making and the Formation of Expectations about Close Relationships," in *Close Relationships*, ed. C. Hendrick (Newbury Park, CA: Sage, 1989); J. H. Harvey et al., "Attribution in the Termination of Close Relationships: A Special Focus on the Account," in *The Emerging Field of Personal Relationships*, eds. R. Gilmour and S. W. Duck (Hillsdale, NJ: Lawrence Erlbaum, 1986); J. H. Harvey, A. L. Weber, and T. L. Orbuch, *Interpersonal Accounts: A Social Psychological Perspective* (Cambridge, MA: Basil Blackwell, 1990).
13. I. Altman and D. Taylor, *Social Penetration Theory*.
14. J. Rempel, J. Holmes, and M. Zanna, "Trust in Close Relationships," *Journal of Personality and Social Psychology* 49 (1985): 95–112.

CHAPTER 4

1. J. L. Hocker and W. Wilmot, *Interpersonal Conflict*, 2nd ed. (Dubuque, IA: Wm. C. Brown, 1985).

2. S. Ting-Toomey, "Toward a Theory of Conflict and Culture," in *Communication, Culture, and Organizational Processes*, eds. W. B. Gundykunst, L. Stewart, and S. Ting-Toomey (Beverly Hills, CA: Sage, 1985).

3. D. Infante and C. Wigely, "Verbal Aggressiveness: An Interpersonal Model and Measure," *Communication Monographs*, 53 (1986): 61–69.

4. D. Infante and C. Wigley, "Verbal Aggressiveness: An Interpersonal Model and Measure," *Communication Monographs* 53 (1986): 61–69.

5. J. C. McCroskey, "Oral Communication Apprehension: A Summary of Recent Theory and Research," *Human Communication Research* 4 (1977): 78–96.

6. K. W. Thomas and R. H. Kilmann, *Thomas-Kilmann Conflict MODE Instrument* (Tuxedo, NY: Viacom, 1974).

7. W. Donahue, M. Deiz, and M. Hamilton, "Coding Naturalistic Negotiation Interaction," *Human Communication Research* 10 (1984): 403–26.

8. D. J. Canary and B. H. Spitzberg, "A Model of the Perceived Competence of Conflict Strategies," *Human Communication Research* 15 (1989): 630–49.